D0793390

Resistance and Survival

Resistance and Survival

Children's Narrative from Central America
and the Caribbean

Ann González

The University of Arizona Press   Tucson

The University of Arizona Press
© 2009 The Arizona Board of Regents
All rights reserved

www.uapress.arizona.edu

Library of Congress Cataloging-in-Publication Data

González, Ann.
    Resistance and survival : children's narrative
from Central America and the Caribbean / Ann González.
        p. cm.
    Includes bibliographical references and index.
    ISBN 978-0-8165-2824-0 (cloth : acid-free paper)
        1. Children's literature, Central American—History
and criticism. 2. Children's literature, Caribbean
(Spanish)—History and criticism. I. Title.
    PQ7472.C48G66 2009
    868.9922008—dc22   2009016353

14   13   12   11   10   09   6   5   4   3   2   1

To the memory of my friend and colleague, Edward Dalley, and to his family, who are inspirations to us all.

Contents

Illustrations

Acknowledgments

The research for this book was funded in part by a Faculty Research Grant from the University of North Carolina Charlotte (2007–2008). I am also grateful to the University for relieving me of teaching and administrative duties for the 2006–2007 academic year to do research in Costa Rica. My special thanks to my department chair, Professor Robert Reimer, who encouraged me to pursue this project, wrote letters of recommendation for me, and carefully read my initial proposals. My gratitude also to Professor Tom Reynolds, dean of the Graduate School, and Professor Jurgen Buchenau, director of the Latin American Studies Program, for their support. My graduate and undergraduate students throughout the years have provided me with ideas and materials, many of which found their way into this book. As always my husband served as my closest reader, editor, and friend whose unconventional thinking about Central American culture continually motivates me to dig deeper. I thank my mother, Dr. Lucy Brashear, for her careful reading of several chapters in the early stages and for her encouragement. Finally, I must thank all of my children, not only for their patience and encouragement, but for their interest in all the stories I used to read to them as they were growing up. Parts of this book have appeared as articles in *Caribe, SECOLAS Annals*, and *Ciberletras*.

Resistance and Survival

1
Introduction
Walking in Reverse/Reading in Reverse

Traditionally, society has used children's literature to help socialize children, whether didactically through moral lessons or by example through stories that show children doing the right thing or what happens to children who do not. The idea that children are subalterns[1] "a partly savage tribe" (Lurie ix), or colonial subjects (Kutzer xvi), voiceless and powerless, in need of colonization, civilization, enlightenment, and (re)formation by adults, therefore, is not a particularly new concept. Children's literature deemed "subversive" in the United States and Britain[2] is most often any literature that has not been chosen or condoned by adults, rebellious stories that resist the good boy/good girl image (Lurie).

Latin American children's literature, however, tends to be subversive in quite another sense. While U.S. and European literatures train their children to become better members of the dominant class (Kutzer), Latin American children, who have a long history of domination, first by Spain and then by the United States, have other lessons to learn: for example, how to resist submission or submit with dignity;[3] how to fight the odds and insist on cultural, if not political, independence; how to get what they want without appearing to do so or without angering the dominant class; how to speak through silence and have the last laugh.

Despite the growing deference to multiculturalism and diversity in contemporary U.S. education (Finazzo; Norton; Harris), writing by Latin Americans continues to be consistently marginalized by the Western canon and publishing industry. Central American and Caribbean literature has been neglected even further by the main centers of cultural production within Latin America: that is, Mexico City, Buenos Aires, and São Paulo. Given this added layer of marginalization, Edward Mullen laments "that few areas of Latin America are so little studied as the Caribbean" (88) and Guatemalan writer and critic Arturo Arias concludes that Central American literature emerges from "la marginalidad de la marginalidad" *Gestos* 11 [the margin of the margin]. Because children's stories tend to be consistently undervalued as "literature,"[4] children's literature from Central America and the Caribbean resides at the periphery of the periphery of the periphery—a triple de-centering that would seem to erase it almost entirely from critical study. Thus, despite the slow climb of children's literature to respectability within the academy and the push from educators to include texts from diverse cultures in public education, the critical analysis of children's literature from Central America and the Caribbean remains sketchy at best.

Most analyses of children's literature from the region in Spanish (e.g., M. Dobles [Costa Rica], Armas [Guatemala], or Elizagaray [Cuba]) are national studies using an educational or normative approach to help teachers choose books for children deemed appropriate by those in a position of authority. In English, beyond the occasional journal arti-cle, there are simply no comprehensive analyses of any regional Latin American children's literature. Unlike the numerous studies that show British imperialistic history or nostalgia for England's lost empire in classic books for children (Kutzer; Richards; McGillis) or the growing numbers of studies of African children's literature and its relationship to British colonial practices (e.g., Khorana or Osa), Latin American chil-dren's literature and its relationship to the colonial and imperial practices of both Spain and the United States have yet to receive much attention.

The low profile of Latin America's children's literature, however, pro-vides a space for writers to introduce alternative views and explana-tions about the periphery into what otherwise tends to be a conservative mainstream educational approach. The combination of the "politically correct" glorification of diversity within public education (i.e., multicul-turalism), the embarrassing lack of basic historical information regard-ing other cultures, and the multitude of stereotypes about the "other" that proliferate in the United States make for an ideal situation for non-traditional stories to make their way into the hands of children without much interference from government entities, publishing houses, or even parents and educators.

Theoretical Perspective

With the fall of the Soviet Union, the end of the Cold War, and the ava-lanche of new technology and information exchange, a global economy, backed by a new invisible form of cybernetic colonialism, has emerged. The twentieth-century scenario of powerful rich nations controlling poorer ones in a colonial relationship is rapidly giving way to an illusive, intangible, non-geographic, non-national global economic structure dominated by technology. Together with increasing information exchange, a new totalizing international homogenization threatens the integrity of regional cultural differences. As the boundaries between nations give way to a more pervasive global culture, the importance of an imagined national identity[5] loses its former appeal and produces a paradoxical effect. Rather than a cohesiveness induced by globalization, a new cohesiveness based on belonging to the immediate community, local culture and ethnicity is emerging within the periphery to maintain a sense of identity. Third world literatures[6] have begun to register and promote these local values and narratives "to draw attention to hybrid, oppositional, local resistance to incorporation in nationally constituted forms" (Emery 137). These responses to colonialism, neocolonialism, and the new globalism depend in part on the dynamic, creative (re)inscription of traditions, myths and autochthonous beliefs, as Salvadoran writer Manlio Argueta explains, "to cover the gaps that originated in colonial domination" (Milan Arias 2).

The esthetic pleasure of the text merges inevitably with its function as a link with the past and a projection into the future. As Osayimwense Osa writes in *African Children's and Youth Literature*, "it is the repository of cultural life of the people and is a major source of education for the young" (136). "History," univocal and official, opens up to multiple histories, "a story among other stories" (Clifford 109) together with the possibility for change. The process of globalization, therefore, like any thesis, generates its own antithesis as people search for belonging within their ethnic and cultural communities instead of within the imposed geopolitical and arbitrary boundaries intrinsic to the creation of nations during colonialism and independence. The growth of hegemony along with its tendency to eradicate singularities and blur the identities of the people it affects is consequently met with continued and continuous resistance—plurivocal, vibrant, and unpredictable.

This effort to reclaim and promote ethnic identities within Latin America and the rest of the third world, however, must be understood not as an obstinate rejection of modernism and economic development but rather as a dynamic response to a new world order, a way to participate with integrity and on local terms in the global market. Intellectuals from the metropolis are finally understanding and interpreting these differences in a more positive light: "For too many years, we have denounced the 'structural heterogeneity' of Latin America as an obstacle to development, without considering that it could foment a much more dense and rich interaction than the desired homogenization" (Lechner 128–129). In this restructuring and reorganization of global relationships and the concomitant reconfigurations of existing worldviews, children's literature has a vital role to play as a repository for the forgotten, a reminder of difference and plurality, a reflection of local cultural identities, and a source of agency and imagination.

The theoretical posture of contemporary literary critics concerned with the cultural production of marginalized groups, voiced persuasively by Gayatri Spivak (Ashcroft 24–28), claims that the subaltern cannot speak, at least, as John Beverly clarifies, the subaltern cannot speak in a way that really matters, "a way that would carry any sort of authority or meaning *for us* without altering the relations of power/knowledge that constitute it as subaltern in the first place" (29; my emphasis). Inherent to the process of colonization and its so-called "civilizing" and modernizing mission is the intrinsic and inevitable suppression of local epistemologies and ways of knowing, that is, alternative ways of understanding, explaining, and constructing the world.

Over time, many of these subaltern ways of knowing have undoubtedly disappeared entirely, like extinct species. Others, however, have adapted through the process of transculturation into hybrid or syncretic forms.[7] Still others abide in local memory and oral tradition waiting for the possibility to be revalued or "restituted," as Walter Mignolo posits, in a time and place where colonial difference can be recognized and border knowledge can be enunciated from new loci:

> [T]he fractured locus of enunciation from a subaltern perspective defines border thinking as a response to colonial difference. . . . The epistemological potential of border thinking is . . . to move beyond Eurocentrism, recognizing the achievements and revealing the conditions for the geopolitics of knowledge in the modern/colonial world—recognizing and revealing the coloniality of power imbedded in the geopolitic of knowledge. (*Local Histories* 319)

The deleterious effects of colonialism, therefore, establish the conditions, sacrifices, and costs for "modernization" to take place. For this reason, Mignolo uses a slash when he refers to the modern/colonial world system. Modernity cannot exist without the structure of colonialism to support it. The coloniality of power, culture and worldview is the necessary condition of the modern world. By discounting knowledge that does not derive from the rational Western tradition that creates modernism, the colonizers, whether internal or external, pre- or post-independence, succeed in equating other systems and worldviews with underdeveloped modes of thought such as barbarism, immaturity, primitivism, or childishness.

In addition, adults who have lived under colonialism have been taught to despise and devalue their own history and to aspire to the identity and the attributes of the dominant class, which by definition they can never attain. As Jamaican writer Michelle Cliff acutely observes: "you believe absolutely in the hegemony of the King's English and the form in which it is meant to be expressed. Or else your writing is not literature; it is folklore and can never be art . . . No reggae spoken here" (13). Costa Rican contemporary writer Carlos Cortés queries in a similar vein: "¿de qué se puede escribir en Costa Rica? Es decir: ¿qué se puede decir de un país en el que no hay nada de qué escribir . . . en el que no pasa nada desde el *big bang*?" (11) [What can one write about in Costa Rica? That is: what can one say about a country in which there is nothing to write about . . . in which nothing has happened since the big bang?]. Clearly, peripheral groups find it difficult, if not impossible, to speak to the metropolis, to "us," but they can and do speak to each other and to their own children (who are even more marginalized than they are), often through oral storytelling, myths, and legends.

In addition, every once in a while someone from the metropolis reaches out to someone from the periphery or vice versa in what I have termed in this study "border interaction," that is, those rare, critical moments of cross-cultural interaction when genuine listening and learning from the "other" take place. It is not so much, then, that marginalized groups cannot speak to the center, but rather that the center does not care to listen or, worse, is incapable of comprehending what it hears from the periphery. People who interact on the border, therefore, function as intermediaries or translators, agents who are able to communicate with both sides.

The goal of this book is to serve in precisely that capacity, as a medium for the kind of border interaction that can facilitate the possibilities for dominance to hear the suppressed and marginalized voices at the periphery. The fundamental objectives, then, that drive this study are to discover what marginalized peoples say when they speak to their children and how these messages may, in fact, be relevant to "us."

Writing in Reverse/Reading in Reverse

Postcolonial critic Ranajit Guha asserts that peasant insurgency in India "inscribed in elite discourse . . . had to be read as a writing in reverse" (qtd. in Beverly 27). Pulin Garg, another postcolonial Indian critic, explains that in order to formulate "a new cultural identity relevant to the times" India must go "backward to go forward" (60). Jamaican writer Michelle Cliff titles one of her books *The Land of Look Behind*. These references to looking backwards or doing things in reverse are recurrent in the thinking and writing of colonial and neocolonial subjects, marginalized and peripheral groups. In addition, the term "backward," as a negative valuation, has frequently been used to describe the third world by imperial powers, as in "backward nations" or "backward societies." The nuances of such a construction are intriguing, reflecting multiple, and clearly, contradictory possibilities. The subtitle of this study, *Reading in Reverse*, therefore, is a metaphor rich in possibilities.

First, neither "backward" nor "forward" is an objective term referring to one particular direction over another. Dominance determines what direction will be termed "forward" as opposed to "backward," what is "forward thinking" as opposed to "backward thinking." By revaluing the term "backward," however, possibilities emerge for movement in other directions than those prescribed by hegemony. As when driving a car in reverse, the same trajectory can be covered but from a new vantage point, a different angle, permitting the driver to see things while going in reverse that he or she missed when going forward. Moving backward also allows for the discovery of wrong turns, permitting the driver/reader the possibility of understanding how the past has led to the present or, in other words, increasing the chances of finding answers to the questions that have nagged at Latin America, questions such as the one Mario Vargas Llosa poses at the opening of his novel *Conversación en la catedral* (1969): "¿En que momento se había jodido el Perú?" [At what point had Peru gone wrong?].

On the one hand, because the discourse of the dominant culture can never claim to represent the "other" accurately, objectively, or with disinterest, the only way for peripheral groups to see themselves in "elite discourse" is to read the opposite or reverse of what is written—to deconstruct, critique, question, and resist the descriptions that dominance would have alterity believe about itself. Thus, reading backwards becomes a metaphor for reading from a critical angle or reading the same "reality" from an oppositional stance. This kind of reading allows the reader to unmask, identify, and deconstruct the assumptions that underpin hegemony—those fundamental constructions that are naturalized to the point that they pass without question. Who is to say, for example, that the direction that hegemony promotes is "forward" or that "forward" is actually the best direction to pursue?

On the other hand, reading in reverse or looking backward points to the need for colonial subjects and marginalized groups to (re)view the past, to understand and reclaim their heritage and cultural ethos in an effort to construct and identify themselves in the present in their own terms outside the parameters of Western thought. This looking behind them chronologically permits the formulation of revisionist history, a critical reading of the past that can liberate the periphery from a Eurocentric master version that determines right from wrong, justified from unjustified, chosen versus imposed.[8] It is also a way of reclaiming the oral tradition, stories from the past that represent local knowledge that has been consistently and systematically destroyed, repressed, or ignored by the colonial need to value itself over its subjects.

Finally, reading in reverse can be seen as an example of doing things backwards, that is, doing things in an unconventional way, which allows peripheral groups to appear unsophisticated (unable to read, reading from right to left) while at the same time permitting them the space to maneuver within the ensuing confusion caused by their deception. One of the unusual attributes of Caribbean and Central American children's narrative is, precisely, its recurrent admiration for astute, trickster characters, who metaphorically know how to read in reverse, that is, those veiled, clever, noncontentious operators who often mask themselves as inadequate, simple, or ingenuous country bumpkins, yet somehow manage to come out on top.

Children from the United States also read about astute characters; in fact, they are taught through literature to root for the underdog. Rooting for the trickster character in Latin American literature, however, is not at all analogous to rooting for the underdog in the United States even though both figures are socially disadvantaged characters who succeed in the end. The American underdog is an individual who, against the odds, achieves success, defined in terms of the American Dream, through perseverance and strength of character. In Latin America, however, the underdog is fundamentally different; he or she is an astute figure whose deceptions represent the unconventional ways that the periphery uses to satisfy basic needs (hunger or survival). Since the ordinary avenues to success within the dominant culture are not available to colonial subjects, they must create their own. Hence, trickster characters and the texts that portray their deceptions in Latin America all find ways to cover their tracks and hide what they do; they speak on multiple, sometimes even contradictory, levels to multiple audiences: children, adults, colleagues, and peers. Yet the message is always fundamentally the same: how to get what is necessary without direct confrontation or open resistance. Central American and Caribbean stories are tales that children learn to read in reverse—that is, they read the omissions, the spaces, the subterfuges of local speech, the magic of the impossible, and the fantasy of liberation.

In the Dominican Republic, for example, a legend exists about a magical people known as the *Ciguapas*. Some versions say they live in trees and only come down in the dark (Bosch); others say they live in the ocean and come out only at night to pick fruit (Álvarez); others claim that they live deep in caves and sneak into houses to steal food (Ubiñas). Still another version claims that the *Ciguapa* is a witch (*bruja*) who lives in the mountains (Langer de Ramírez). All of the versions, however, coincide on one main point: the *Ciguapas* have feet that point backwards. The footprints that the *Ciguapas* leave appear to go in the opposite direction from their true path (see fig. 1.1). Anyone trying to find them will logically go the wrong way.

There is good reason for such an unusual anatomy—walking backwards is a mythical modification that permits survival. On an island where the Spanish decimated the entire indigenous population shortly after the conquest, the mythical invention of a group who managed to survive must have been a psychological imperative. The legend of the *Ciguapas*, therefore, and its perpetuation in contemporary Dominican literature for children (cf. Blanco Díaz, Ng, or Miller-Lachmann), reveal the existence in myth of a marginalized culture, a fictional invention that propagates an ingenious and active form of resistance. Paradoxically, the *Ciguapas* exemplify both the plight of the subaltern—mute, hidden, mysterious, Other—as well as successful subversion. Walking in reverse becomes a metaphor, like reading in reverse, for a form of duplicity that offers a space for resistance inside the dominant codes.

Figure 1.1. Footprints of the Ciguapa leading back to the ocean in a version of the Dominican folktale retold by Julia Álvarez, illustrated by Fabián Negrín (2000). Reprinted, courtesy of the publisher, Random House.

The Objective of This Study

Mexican writer and critic Carlos Fuentes was one of the first to point out that Latin American writers have always taken on the responsibility to speak for those with no voice, often encoding their messages to circumvent censorship and political oppression. Children's literature in the region, therefore, functions as an ideal medium and locus from which to enunciate unorthodox ideas, reclaim local epistemologies, and interject the ethos of local cultural identities into the dominant discourse. The objective of this study, therefore, is to uncover these "fractured enunciations" (Mignolo, *Local Histories*) and "introjections" (Garg) in an attempt to redeem the suppressed and marginalized "knowledges" that colonial powers have repeatedly and systematically discounted or effaced throughout Central America and the Caribbean.

Part of this task is to reveal not only those ideas that a writer intends to include for the socialization of children, but also to deconstruct those unintended messages that may reflect his or her implicit acceptance of the hegemonic values and social codes of a particular cultural or historical moment, indeed a pervasive and underlying ideology that may be at odds with the writer's own explicit beliefs and perspective. These tensions between "the coloniality of power," that is, the darker side of the civilizing and modernizing mission of colonialism, and "the colonial difference," or the recognition of the epistemic violence (Spivak) and suppression that such "civilization" and "modernization" inevitably entails, are particularly apparent in children's literature from the region.

While the goal of this study is to look critically at works written for children, or later adapted for children, by important Central American and Caribbean writers, it is not intended to be a comprehensive survey or overview of children's works from the region. Rather, it is a critical analysis of representative cases beginning with Cuban revolutionary José Martí's famous collection for children *La edad de oro* in 1889 and ending with an evaluation of the contemporary writing that is emerging from Costa Rica, a Central American country long admired for its emphasis on education. Through close textual readings, each essay exposes and decodes the polyphonic voices and subversive messages that are masked either intentionally or at a subliminal level in selected works for children from this region. The general approach, which locates each work both in historical context and within the context of the writer's entire corpus, derives from cultural studies and postcolonial narrative theory and examines not only the discourse but also in some instances the artistic techniques in the illustrations that reflect and reveal dominant value systems or their subversions.

Writers from as many of the countries in the area as possible are included, but inevitably some countries have been left out and others have received more than their share of attention. Costa Rica's children's literature, for example, is the most thoroughly analyzed, starting with Carmen Lyra's stories at the beginning of the twentieth century, followed by Joaquín Gutiérrez's famous novel for children at mid-century and ending with a review of three contemporary writers from the country. The reason is simple; Costa Rica is the country with which I have had the most contact over the last thirty years. The choice of authors has been based less on their country of origin and more on their regional significance, their impact on the educational system, their role in cultural identity formation, and their reflection of changing worldviews. Ultimately, as the concept of nation becomes less important in the new age of globalism, those writers who reflect the cultural identity and concerns of the region grow more important. The generalized class consciousness of Central America and the Caribbean as peripheral areas of the Americas that must struggle to maintain their basic existence is encoded systematically in the literature for children from Martí forward.

As for the always polemical discussion as to what children's literature actually is or even if it exists at all as a discrete category, for my purposes here, I have adopted the position that if the author or editorial company has aimed the narrative at children, or if parents, educators, or children themselves have appropriated the work, then the text can be discussed as a manifestation of children's literature.

The Essays

The first essay on Martí, one of the few Hispanic authors whose work for children has received considerable academic attention, looks closely at how Martí talks about gender, race, and the "other" in his revolutionary magazine, *La edad de oro* (1889), written for the Spanish-speaking children of the Americas. It concludes that the dominant ideological biases of his day have permeated his thinking, despite his explicit calls for liberation and equality. It also indicates how Martí's language has set the standard for a kind of egalitarian dialogue with the reader, whatever age he or she might be.

The next essay on Costa Rica's foundational figure in children's literature, Carmen Lyra, argues that her famous book for children, *Cuentos de
mi tía Panchita* (1920), has been and continues to be instrumental in the
process of Costa Rican national and cultural identity formation, based
on a subtle rejection of colonial Eurocentric models. Between the lines
and often in the guise of fairy tales and folk legends, she posits a hidden
astuteness that drives her superficially simple protagonists who repeatedly manage to get the better of more powerful opponents. Her call to
value local artistic production and thought radically subverts the colonial and neocolonial beliefs in the superiority of all things European.

The chapter on Puerto Rico's feminist icon Rosario Ferré attempts
to broaden the study of her work by looking past isolated gender issues
to the more complex issues of racial, social, and political power struggles reflected in her various stories for children. Her collection for young
readers *Sonatinas* (1989) contains multiple subversions of the dominant colonial/neocolonial ideology that inevitably undervalues and sup-
presses local cultural resources, including women.

The study on Costa Rican novelist Joaquín Gutiérrez documents and
analyzes the major public controversy that surfaced in 2003 when the
then minister of education declared *Cocorí* (1949), Gutiérrez's popular
story for children, a racist novel. This essay, like the chapter on Martí,
studies the gaps and contradictions between a writer's intentions and a
reader's construction of meaning. It also links to the chapter on Lyra by
analyzing the changing images of national/cultural identity along with
Costa Rica's simultaneous and contradictory admiration for and rejection of Western culture.

The chapter on El Salvador's Manlio Argueta provides an allegorical
and politico-historical reading of his story for children *Los perros mágicos
de los volcanes* (1990) and emphasizes his role in the inscription of the popular oral tradition of the region. The essay also documents how the story
has penetrated the heart of hegemony through its recent publication in a
bilingual edition and how the story has been promoted by multicultural
educators in the United States apparently unaware of its politically subversive content.

Nicaraguan poet and novelist Gioconda Belli's story for children *El
taller de las mariposas* (1994) is a text with multiple layers and multiple audiences: children, adults, fellow Sandinistas, and fellow writers. Its
complexity is further exacerbated by the inclusion of subversive illustrations that turn Christian cosmology on its head and posit a utopia

based on consensus and the cultivation of the imagination. In addition, this essay points out underlying parallels and contraditions between her famous compatriot Rubén Darío's modernist aesthetics and Belli's ideas about the creation of art.

The final chapter looks at Costa Rica's three most prominent contemporary writers, Lara Ríos, Carlos Rubio, and the current minister of education, Leonardo Garnier. Their challenge as children's writers has been to mediate between an inherently fractured, complex postmodern world and a child's individual experience. As Costa Rica finds itself at risk of being swallowed up in a global drive to embrace broadening economic markets and technological advances, these writers manage to transmit the value of local and personal meaning in an effort to reclaim the margins and redefine cultural identity. These are astute writers, like the astute characters they portray, who are well aware of their peripheral status and the increasing sophistication of their readers, and who understand that their books must compete with television, video games, and computerized audiovisual media, as well as the traditional canon and the powerful lure of children's literature produced in the metropolis and translated for foreign consumption. As part of my research for this chapter I interviewed Leonardo Garnier, Costa Rica's minister of education, in June 2007.

The book concludes with an analysis of the Caribbean folk hero, Juan Bobo—Juan, the region's Everyman, and Bobo, a synonym in Spanish for simpleminded. Through this traditional character who seems to do everything backwards but who still manages, in the worst of the cases to get his way and in the best to become "king," the metaphor from the title of this chapter "reading in reverse" comes full circle. Here is a character who represents a genuinely alternative vision and an "other" way of functioning that defies and resists hegemony's expectations. Questions of cultural identity and self-esteem merge with humor, dissimulation, and, often, plain dumb luck to form a complex imaginary that has helped the region survive not only an excruciatingly painful conquest and colonial history, but also an intimidating and terrifying global assimilation.

2
In the Beginning
José Martí and *La edad de oro*

Contrary to the forgotten and invisible status of Latin American children's literature generally, *La edad de oro* (1889) by José Martí (1853–1895), dedicated to the children of the Americas, has received an uncommon amount of critical attention from his day to ours. The numerous studies can be broken down into three major areas: (1) analyses of language, style, and structure, particularly the modernist aesthetics at work in his texts (Larrea; Lolo, "José Martí" and *Mar de Espuma*; Serna Arnaiz; Fraser; López Terrero), (2) Martí's sociopolitical ideas, especially regarding government, patriotism, the essential brotherhood of man, and the equality of all races (Jiménez, Cruz, Pérez, Hernández Biosca), and finally, (3) Martí's educational philosophy and pedagogical approach (Izquierdo Miller; Klein; Matthews; Hernández-Miyares; Foner; Cerezal; Gallego Alfonso, "Apuntes" and "Para un estudio"). With such a large body of critical literature on Martí (almost nine hundred titles appear in the *Modern Language Association Bibliography* alone), I hesitate to offer yet another study. Still, an analysis of the important works for children to emerge from Central America and the Caribbean would be incomplete—indeed could not really begin—without including the foundational figure of Cuba's Martí.

José Martí is particularly important since he was one of the first intellectual activists from Spanish-speaking America to point out the negative effects of colonialism, the dangers of neocolonialism, and the importance of valuing autochthonous history and knowledge.[1] A precursor of the most important movement in aesthetics to originate in the New World, *Modernismo*, and an ardent spokesperson for the independence of Cuba (he lost his life fighting against the Spanish troops on the island), Martí was an authentic Renaissance man, "un hombre total" (Torres Rioseco 282) [a total man]. Chilean poet and Nobel laureate Gabriela Mistral called him a cultured Adam, impressed with his "mixture of vast information and constant originality" (Fernández Retamar,).

In fact, his interest in and dedication to children would seem almost out of character[2] were it not for his firm belief that any possibilities for socio-political change ultimately depended on the next generations.[3]

While he lived in New York, Martí published only four issues of the magazine *La edad de oro* (variously translated as "The Golden Age" or "The Gilded Age") from July to October 1889, before abruptly discontinuing it. He wrote in a letter to a friend in Mexico that he had disagreed with the editor and owner/financial backer, Brazilian Antonio Da Costa Gómez, regarding content—"quería el editor que yo hablase del 'temor de Dios'" (qtd. in Lolo, *Mar de Espuma* 20) [the editor wanted me to talk about the 'fear of God']. It is still not clear, however, why Da Costa Gómez would have withheld such radically didactic intentions until after the publication of the first issues.[4] Moreover, the magazine appeared to be a financial success; it had been well publicized and marketed, and there was virtually no competition in Spanish. Magazines for children in English and French were popular at the time, but beyond some Spanish translations of the Grimm's brothers and some fables from Spain, nothing before Martí had been aimed specifically at Spanish-speaking children in North and South America (see Schultz de Mantovani or A. Rodríguez). Since Martí was the sole author of the material included and he already had an established reputation as a writer for adults,[5] the publication was virtually guaranteed a substantial reading public both in North and South America. To the surprise of Cuban exiles at the time, even the Spanish colonial government in Cuba permitted distribution of the magazine.

Although Da Costa himself came up with the title for *La edad de oro*, Martí's subtitle offers some insight into his motives for taking on this enterprise: *Publicación Mensual de Recreo e Instrucción, Dedicada a los Niños de América* [Monthly Publication of Recreation and Instruction, Dedicated to the Children of America] (see fig. 2.1). In addition, a letter he writes to his friend Mercado about this new project reiterates the importance of promoting citizenship among young people so that they may know and live productively in the land in which they were born: "A nuestros niños los hemos de criar para hombres de su tiempo y hombres de América. Si no hubiera tenido a mis ojos esta dignidad, yo no habría entrado en esta empresa" (qtd. in Gallego Alfonso 166) [We should rear our children to be men of their time and men of America. Had I not had this dignified goal before me, I would not have tackled this enterprise].

Figure 2.1. The front cover from the first issue of *La edad de oro* by José Martí (1889). Artist unknown.

Following Aristotle's belief that literature should both entertain and instruct,[6] Martí deftly interweaves his didactic/moral lessons into the overall entertainment of the magazine hoping, like Mary Poppins, that a spoonful of sugar will help the medicine go down: "de manera que . . . contribuya todo en cada número directo y agradablemente a la instrucción ordenada y útil de nuestros niños y niñas" (qtd. in Lolo, *Mar de Espuma* 14) [such that everything in each issue contributes directly and agreeably to the ordered and useful instruction of our boys and girls]. His intentions are to convey the overriding values of Americanism and liberalism, freedom, friendship, and social equality, ideas that he paints into the "imágenes prístinas" (Lolo, *Mar de Espuma* 10) [pristine images] embraced by modernist aesthetics. His Promethean goals, the liberation of Cuba from Spanish empire and the construction of a Cuban nation, are also persistent leitmotifs. No teaching opportunity is bypassed—in the midst of retelling the stories in Homer's *Iliad*,[7] he remarks:

> En la *Iliada*, aunque no lo parece, hay mucha filosofía, y mucha ciencia, y mucha política, y se enseña a los hombres, como sin querer, que los dioses no son en realidad más que poesías de la imaginación, y que los países no se pueden gobernar por el capricho de un tirano, sino por el acuerdo y respeto de los hombres principales que el pueblo escoge para explicar el modo con que quiere que lo gobiernen. (37)

> [In the *Iliad*, although it may not seem so, there is a great deal of philosophy, science, and politics, and it teaches humankind, almost without meaning to, that gods are in reality only poems of the imagination, and that countries cannot be governed by the whim of a tyrant, but rather by the agreement and respect of the principal leaders that the people choose to explain the way in which they wish to be governed.]

Emulating this strategy, Martí interweaves his convictions and philosophical views on the essence of humanity (a pan-humanism) into each of the texts he includes in *La edad de oro*. In a long article about dwellings from prehistoric times to the present, he concludes like Homer "como sin querer" [almost without meaning to]: "el hombre es el mismo en todas partes, y aparece y crece de la misma manera, y hace y piensa las mismas cosas, sin más diferencia que la de la tierra en que vive" (56) [people are the same everywhere, and they appear and grow in the same way, and they do and think the same things, without any other difference than the land in which they live].

Despite his pedagogical motives and stated intentions for this children's magazine, critics note a major difference between *La edad de oro* and the typical didactic literature popular at the time, a difference that hinges on Martí's unusual respect for children and the relationship he foments between himself as friend/narrator and his implied reader. Hernández-Miyares remarks that "no se percibe aniñamiento alguno, ni tampoco presunción de estilo" (17) [there is no perception of talking down to the child, nor of any presumption of style]. His language is carefully chosen as Martí himself explains in a letter to his daughter María[8]:

> Yo no recuerdo, entre los que tú puedes tener a mano, ningún libro escrito en este español simple y puro. Yo quise escribir así en *La Edad de Oro*, para que los niños me entendieran y el lenguaje tuviera sentido y música. (qtd. in Larrea 4)

> [I don't recall, among those books you might have at hand, any book written in this simple and pure Spanish. I tried to write that way in *La Edad de Oro*, so that children would understand me and the language would have meaning and music.]

Matthews calls Martí's approach to children in *La edad de oro* a "dialogue"[9] and claims that Martí speaks on equal terms with his child reader: "Niños a los que se supone tanto o más hábiles que el propio autor y con los que se trata de conversar de igual a igual" (2) [Children who he supposes are as capable or more so than the author himself and with whom he tries to converse as equals]. In this respect, Martí's style contributes to this sense of equality—long sentences strung together with simile after simile, piling on more and more images, one after the other, much as children tend to do in their oral storytelling. The following quotation from Martí's essay on elephants, for example, only one sentence long, is representative:

> Lo que le gusta es el vino bueno, y el arrak, que es el ron de la India, tanto que los cornacs le conocen el apetito, y cuando quieren que trabaje más de lo de costumbre, le enseñan una botella de arrak, que él destapa con la trompa luego, y bebe a sorbo tendido; sólo que el cornac tiene que andar con cuidado, y no hacerle esperar la botella mucho,

porque le puede suceder lo que al pintor francés que, para pintar a un
elefante mejor, le dijo a su criado que se lo entretuviese con la cabeza
alta tirándole frutas a la trompa, pero el criado se divertía haciendo
como que echaba al aire fruta sin tirarla de veras, hasta que el elefante
se enojó, y se le fue encima a trompazos al pintor, que se levantó del
suelo medio muerto, y todo lleno de pinturas. (151)

[What he likes is good wine and arrak, the rum of India, so much
that the trainers know and when they want the elephant to work
more than usual, they show him a bottle of arrak that the elephant
will uncork later and drink in one huge swallow; only the trainer has
to be careful and not make him wait for the bottle too long because
the same thing might happen that happened to a French painter who
in order to paint the elephant better told his trainer to keep the elephant's head high by throwing fruit up at his trunk, but the trainer
thought it was funny to pretend he was throwing the fruit up without
really throwing it until the elephant got mad and started to beat the
painter with his trunk, and the painter staggered up half dead and all
smeared in paint.]

The "and then, and then" of children's orality is mirrored here in Martí's
string of repetitions in the same breathless enthusiasm of the child, with
the difference, of course, that his masterful choice and recycling of images
divides his narration up into blocks or vignettes and reflects his conscious manipulation of language, a hallmark of modernist aesthetics.

This illusion of a conversation between equals that Martí engineers,
reveals his projection of the child as "other," that is, a figure different from
himself but to whom he assigns the same ontological essence. Fraser
attributes this attitude to Martí's modernist aestheticism that claims "the
superiority of the child's perspective to that of the uncomprehending
adult world" (226). Matthews notes, for example, that children in Martí
have "sus propias posibilidades, como una forma de ir más allá de la
razón adulta" (2) [their own possibilities, as a way of going beyond adult
reasoning]. Thus, Martí sees the child not only as "other" but also as "una
alternativa válida" (Matthews 2) [a valid alternative], who deserves his
utmost respect. His pedagogy, consequently, deconstructs the traditional
stance of superior adult to inferior child, and initiates instead a two-way
exchange, familiar, friendly, and oral. His intentions, ultimately, are not
so much to teach the child as to persuade a friend:

este proyecto educativo-cultural, proyecto guiado primordialmente por un genuino amor a la niñez Americana y el deseo de prepararla y convertirla en la fuente generadora de ciudadanos cabales para un futuro luminoso. (Hernández-Miyares 17)

[this educational-cultural project guided primarily by a genuine love for American children and the desire to prepare them and transform them into a generative fountain of whole and complete citizens for a bright future.]

Children, however, have the uncanny (and irritating) ability to learn what we least mean to teach and to hear what we have no intention of saying. Only a small percentage of communication is verbal and even language itself reflects the dominant ideology and cultural conventions that surround us. Children learn to read what is absent as well as what is present, thus the metaphor I have used throughout this collection of "reading in reverse." What interests me here, therefore, is not so much the liberal, modernist program that Martí clearly intends to weave into his discourse—a subject that many critics have already studied—but the underlying and contradictory elements in colonialist ideology that, despite Martí's overwhelming and conscious efforts to resist, make their way into the text like the symbolic neocolonial tiger from Martí's most famous essay "Nuestra América" that "vuelve de noche al lugar de la presa" [returns at night to the site of its prey].

Despite Martí's insistence that changing the outward forms of colonial control would be unsuccessful if the spirit of government did not also change, he was not fundamentally a social revolutionary or reformer. He was above all a liberator, like Bolívar and San Martín before him. Thus, his discourse on liberation does not question the essential structural conditions inherited from the colonial empire. Those colonial prescriptions of internal control continue to regulate the structure of societies under the process of liberation from external controls.

One example of this limitation in the scope of Martí's liberation efforts is his view of women as caretakers. While a proponent of female education, a fairly unorthodox position at the time, he clearly visualizes women within the private sphere of home and family. His view that "Las niñas deben saber lo mismo que los niños, para poder hablar con ellos como amigos" (11) [girls should know the same things as boys so that they can talk to them as partners] intends to strengthen a woman's role at home as friend and intellectual companion to her husband: "es una pena que el hombre tenga que salir de su casa a buscar con quien hablar, porque las mujeres de la casa no sepan contarle más que de diversiones y de modas" (11) [it's a pity that a man has to leave his house to find someone to talk to because the women at home don't know anything to talk about other than entertainment and fashion]. As Foner observes:

> Not a very radical approach to female education, to be sure, but considering the fact that it was as yet a rarity in Latin America for women to attend colleges and universities, the attention Martí paid to female education in the United States in his dispatches to the Latin American press contributed to advancing the concept that such education was in the best interest of the nation. (19)

As revolutionary as his ideas about gender may have been for the last third of the nineteenth century, they often seem like an afterthought in his overall vision of equality: "Para los niños es este periódico, y para las niñas, por supuesto" (Martí 9) [This magazine is for boys, and for girls, of course]. His very punctuation indicates that he has added girls onto an already formulated idea. He goes on in his introductory letter in *La edad de oro* to explain all about a writing competition he plans to have and to request that the boys send him letters and ask questions. Remembering he has not specified that all these activities are also for girls, he adds almost patronizingly, "Las niñas también pueden escribirnos sus cartas, y preguntarnos cuanto quieran saber, y mandarnos sus composiciones para la competencia de cada seis meses. ¡De seguro que van a ganar las niñas!" (12) [Girls can also write us letters and ask us anything they want to know, and send us their compositions for the contest every six months. Without doubt, the girls will win!] His assurance that the girls will win the competition sounds strangely condescending and unconvincing, added on at the last minute so as not to offend.

His position that "la niña nace para madre" (9) [girls are born to be mothers], however, is more disturbing. As Marx pointed out, the first form of slavery was the result of this biological imperative that drove the division of labor, leaving women at home while men accrued power in the public sphere. Marx's solution to this conundrum is irrelevant. The point is that by espousing a Darwinian based, biologically driven philosophical posture, which underlies the modern nineteenth-century worldview, Martí precludes any possibility for women to become equal partners in the liberation project.

Cruz argues that the entire subject of gender in Martí has been subsumed under his idealist image and that this mythification of Martí as "Cuban hero" has prevented a hard look at any aspect of his work that might prove critical to his larger-than-life status. She even goes so far as to claim that "por debajo de una aparente veneración de la mujer, subyace en la poesía y la prosa de José Martí una intensa corriente misógina" (30) [beneath the apparent veneration of women in the poetry and prose of José Martí lies an intense misogynist vein]. Such a conclusion should not, by any means, be interpreted as diminishing the image of Martí, the idealist and liberator, but rather serves to remind us that he is, after all, a man of history. That is, he emerges from a particular time and place and is subject to the naturalized and pervasive assumptions about gender that the dominant ideology and the society it has created espouse. As Maldonado and others have pointed out, Martí was as radical as he could be for the historical moment in which he lived: "luchó por hacer, para su circunstancia, lo más radical que el proceso histórico le permitía" (Maldonado 192) [he fought to make, for his circumstances, the most radical changes that the historical process would permit]. To criticize Martí for a lack of vision or foresight regarding such a controversial topic as gender is to make a completely anachronistic criticism, easy to do in hindsight, but fundamentally unfair.

Gender, however, is not the only area where the dominant ideology filters into Martí's discourse. A close look at his original stories and poems in La edad de oro indicates contradictions and ambivalences hidden inside Martí's revolutionary ideas. "La muñeca negra," for example, published in the fourth issue, ostensibly emphasizes Martí's beliefs in racial equality and subtly critiques the comfortable bourgeoisie who would forget the marginalized and downtrodden and insulate themselves from the realities of poverty and injustice that surround them. Piedad, a beautiful little white girl about to celebrate her eighth birthday, loves her old black doll, Leonor. Piedad's parents, who represent a typical bourgeois marriage (stay-at-home mom, hard working, and mostly absent father), give their daughter a new porcelain doll dressed in silk and lace for her birthday. After playing a while with the new doll, Piedad, claiming she is sleepy, asks to be sent to bed early so that she can cuddle with her old doll, Leonor, whom she favors. Martí's purposeful message is clear: we should identify and love the "other," the marginalized, poor, and disadvantaged, "amor por lo sencillo, por lo supuestamente simple, amor ante todo hacia el hombre sin distinción de clase o color" (Pozo Campos 130) [love for the unassuming, for the supposedly simple, love above all toward people without distinction of class or color]. The element of race is suggested[10] subtly but unequivocally in the central symbol of the black doll.

Underneath this idealistic message and certainly contrary to any "meaning" that Martí intends to convey, however, is a disturbing undercurrent of colonialist attitudes. First and clearest is Martí's apparent acceptance and confirmation of Western, Eurocentric standards of beauty. Piedad is beautiful with her hair as golden as the sun; her new white doll with its blond hair and blue eyes is beautiful; but Leonor, the black doll with her faded features and ragged appearance, is not: "Mamá . . . dice que te he puesto muy fea con tantos besos, y que no tienes pelo, porque te he peinado mucho!" (Martí 144) [Mama says that I've made you ugly from so many kisses and that you don't have hair because I've combed it so much].

This description of the beautiful white child, contrasted to another less fortunate child (in this case doll) is not unique in *La edad de oro*. In another of Martí's stories in the collection "Bebé y el señor Don Pomposo" published in the first issue, Martí offers a similar description: "Bebé es un niño magnífico, de cinco años. Tiene el pelo muy rubio, que le cae en rizos por la espalda" (49) [Bebé is a magnificent little boy aged five. He has very blond hair that falls in curls down his back]. His orphaned cousin Raúl is portrayed, not only as Bebé's opposite, but as a child who is lacking[11]: "un primito suyo que *no tiene* madre . . . el *pobre* Raúl . . . *no tiene* el pelo rubio, *ni* va vestido de duquesito, *ni* lleva medias de seda colorada" (50; emphasis mine) [a little cousin of his who *doesn't have* a mother . . . *poor* Raul . . . he *doesn't have* blond hair, *nor* is he dressed like a little duke, *nor* does he wear colorful silk stockings]. Despite Martí's overt message of equality, therefore, we are reminded of the Western ideal of human beauty: white skin, blond hair, and blue eyes, without which one is somehow incomplete or deficient.

In his essay from the fourth issue in the collection, "Un paseo por la tierra de los anamitas," Martí waffles back and forth on the subject. At first, he indicates that standards of beauty are products of cultural determinations, not innate qualities (that is, we do not all agree on what is beautiful) when he claims that the Vietnamese, "los ananitas": "[n]o nos parecen de cuerpo hermoso, ni nosotros les parecemos hermosos a ellos" (128) [Physically, they do not seem beautiful to us, nor do we appear beautiful to them]. Clearly, he is aware of cultural differences regarding aesthetics. Still, he reminds us later in *their* voice: "somos amarillos, chatos, canijos, y feos" (130) [we are yellow, short, weak, and ugly]. Although the "other," that is, the "ananita," is technically speaking here, the voice identifies and judges itself based on Eurocentric views, despite Martí's having indicated earlier that the Vietnamese might not see themselves as we see them.

This discourse is at odds with itself. On the one hand, Martí admires the Vietnamese and consciously desires to persuade his readers of their innate value as people by describing their many accomplishments and historical fortitude. On the other, he judges their beauty based on the unstated assumptions of white superiority. Martí's neocolonial tiger has struck again: "comienza entonces un proceso sistemático de alienación colectiva que convierte al colonizado en un ser para quien lo suyo resulta extraño y lo extraño parece suyo" (Maldonado 195) [A systematic process begins of collective alienation that converts the colonized person into a being for whom his own seems foreign and what is foreign seems his]. This inversion, when the "ananita" judges himself ugly in comparison to Westerners, reflects the power of colonialist ideology to impose its standards, in this case the standards for beauty, on the colonized (both Martí and the "ananitas"). The ugliness that Martí sees in the "other"—whether African or Asian, or simply not blond—reflects an implicit, albeit, unconscious, sense of white superiority that colonialism inculcates,[12] a notion that Martí clearly and consciously rejects in all of his writings both for children and adults, but an assumption to which he falls victim himself in his consistent descriptions of beautiful white children with blue eyes and blond curls.

The undercurrent of white superiority that lurks beneath Martí's clearest claims to the contrary, also parallels the general nineteenth-century belief in male superiority. Cruz notes, for example, that Martí often sets up a moral opposition between the sexes "entre los 'galanes blancos' y las 'Venus negras'" (31) [between the white handsome male and the black Venus]. The binomial oppositions that value the first term over the second are consistent: white/black, moral/immoral, male/female.

These fundamental assumptions are an inevitable consequence of Martí's faith in humankind's linear and temporal progress (evolution) resulting from scientific achievement and advancement: "Martí reconoce abiertamente su admiración creciente con los descubrimientos de Darwin y su creencia en el progreso de la ciencia" (Jiménez 150)

[Martí openly recognizes his growing admiration for Darwin's discoveries and his belief in the progress of science]. Although he insists that all people are equal and essentially alike, different societies, he explains, are to be found around the globe at various stages of cultural development: "donde nace el hombre salvaje, sin saber que hay ya pueblos en el mundo, empieza a vivir lo mismo que vivieron los hombres de hace miles de años" (56) [where man is born wild, without knowing that there are already other peoples in the world, he begins to live the same way that people lived thousands of years ago]. That is, where people first appeared (Europe), they developed first, and for this reason we see them as more advanced: "como que allí empezó a vivir, allí fue donde llegó más pronto a saber, y a descubrir los metales, y a fabricar" (59) [since people began to live there, they came to know earlier and to discover metals and build]. This superiority, according to Martí, is the product of time, not the result of inherent, ontological or biological characteristics. Thus, while he continues to champion the equality of all peoples, he never questions the superiority of Europe to the rest of the world.

His attempt to explain cultural differences through a belief in a linear and progressive development of humanity inevitably buys into the colonialist assumption of racial superiority. Although he makes a heroic effort to value local knowledge through his descriptions of the indigenous cultural achievements of the Americas and to invert Sarmiento's famous civilization versus barbarism opposition by showing the Spanish as the true barbarians of the conquest, his fundamental confidence in progress and development through incremental stages, that is, his belief in the underlying progressive paradigm of the nineteenth century,[13] subverts any real possibility for promoting a paradigm of equality. The two paradigms are mutually exclusive in their underlying views of the "development" of humanity and the value of local histories, knowledges, and wisdoms. Martí would have us believe that some cultures simply have to "catch up" to others. The unstated assumption in this game of "catch up," however, is that these cultures are not just different from ours, but subaltern, "other," and inferior, lacking in the accumulated knowledge of "civilized" peoples.

This implicit underdevelopment emerges in another form in Martí's "La muñeca negra" where Piedad's love for her black doll emanates, not from any essential sense of justice or equality, but rather from a sense of pity. She reiterates her love for Leonor (echoes of Poe) at various moments in the story "te quiero mucho, porque no te quieren" (144, 146)

[I love you very much, because they don't love you]. Indeed, her reason for loving Leonor is stated in the last line of the story—a structurally significant and forceful place to locate the overriding theme—a theme, I would argue, that is hardly a declaration of equality.

Acting out of pity assumes a sense of superiority on the part of the actor. In fact, this asymmetrical compassion for the "other" reenacts the same rationalization process of colonialism itself. As Maldonado explains:

> Lo que el colonizador hace, una vez que valida su presencia mediante un acto de fuerza, es pretender racionalizar dicho acto invocando que es él el portador del fuego civilizador, y que su labor Prometeica es un sacrificio auto-impuesto para el beneficio—no de él, desde luego— sino del colonizado. (195)

> [What the colonizer does, once he validates his presence by way of an act of force, is to pretend to rationalize his acts by claiming that he is the bearer of the flame of civilization and that his Promethean labor is a sacrifice he has placed on himself for the benefit—not of himself, of course—but of the colonized.]

That is, the colonizer's pity for these inferior others who lack civilization and knowledge of the "true religion," adequate health care, or economic development, whatever the current buzz word may be, motivates and justifies the colonizer's actions, interventions, and intromissions. What intends to pass as "sharing" with the other, when motivated by pity, is ultimately imposition. Yet Martí seems not to recognize this very situation and its possible similarities to Cuba's fight for liberation from Spain, when he tells the story of "Gordon el chino, que no era chino, sino muy blanco y de ojos muy azules" [Gordon the Chinaman, who was not Chinese but very white with very blue eyes], an English governor in Sudan who controlled the people "sin más armas que sus ojos azules" [with no other arms than his blue eyes] and who would "regañarlos como a hijos" [scold them like children] and "llorar de piedad por los negros" [cry out of pity for the blacks]. The intentional image Martí paints of Gordon is that of "un inglés muy valiente" [a courageous Englishman] instead of the patriarchal and patronizing colonialist governor that emerges from this description. Martí seems not to know which side he is backing—Gordon and his blue eyes or "el Mahdí," "un peleador famoso" [a famous fighter], and the black rebels who gather in the mountains "a ver como atacarían a los hombres blancos" (148) [to see how to attack the white men]. His conclusion is noncommittal: "dicen que Gordon ha muerto, o lo tiene preso el Mahdí" (148) [they say Gordon has died or that he is being held prisoner by the Mahdí]. The fact that Gordon is not a cruel governor but one of the European "hombres buenos" [good men] does not make him any less an extension of the same colonial power that Martí decries so forcefully on other occasions. Somehow Gordon's goodness, courage, pity (and blue eyes) justify his position.

Piedad's declarations of love for her black doll function in the same way. Her love is motivated by compassion. Martí reminds his readers through Piedad's very name (which signifies *pity*)[14] that this emotion underscores the text. Martí obviously does not perceive the negative undercurrents associated with the concept. Indeed, he consciously values and intends to cultivate this attribute in his young readers. Yet, feeling sorry for others, that is, the sentiment we call pity, can be expressed only for those who are in some way inferior or, like Raúl in "Bebé y el señor Don Pomposo," those who are lacking: less fortunate, less wealthy, less beautiful, less intelligent, less healthy, less capable, less loved. Compassion should not be confused with empathy, feeling what others feel, or sympathy, understanding what others feel; sentiments that achieve subject/object identification without devaluing the objective "other" in relation to the subject.

Pity, however, is an emotion that Martí ably manipulates to motivate generosity in his characters as well as in his readers. Piedad loves her black doll precisely because no one else does. Bebé lays his new saber on the pillow of the sleeping Raúl precisely because Raúl does not have one, nor does he have any of the material possessions or attributes that Bebé has been taught to value. Nevertheless, Martí's clearest depiction of pity at work can be found in his famous narrative poem "Los zapaticos de rosa," published in the third issue of *La edad de oro*. Pilar, the little white rich girl of the poem (from the *pillar* of society) gives her new pink shoes to another child who is poor and sick and barefoot: "¡Oh, toma, toma los míos:/Yo tengo más en mi casa!" (124) [Oh, take them, take mine: I have more at home!]. Pilar's mother, who is about to scold her daughter for losing her shoes at the beach, is stopped by the mother of the sick girl who gives an account of Pilar's generosity. Pilar's mother reacts in much the same way as her daughter does, although as an adult, she is more consciously guilty for having so many material possessions in the face of such poverty: "'¡Sí, Pilar, dáselo! ¡y eso/También! ¡tu manta! ¡tu anillo!'" (124) [Yes, Pilar, give it to her! And that, also! Your blanket! Your ring!]. Guilt, combined with pity, motivates the benevolence of the characters.

The story is literally a tearjerker; other tourists at the beach, overhearing the two mothers' conversation, start to cry: "Se vio sacar los pañuelos/A una rusa y a una inglesa;/El aya de la francesa/ Se quitó los espejuelos" (124) [A Russian and an English lady took out their handkerchiefs; the French girl's tutor took off her spectacles]. The elements in the situation are stocks in trade for provoking reader pity—a sick child, a poor mother—Disney could do no better. But the psychological mechanism at play here is based upon guilt in the face of such unequal material prosperity—a child who can spare a pair of shoes since she has others at home versus a child so poor that she has no shoes at all.

Martí is not averse to relying on such stock situations to garner compassion for the poor and marginalized. In fact, he manipulates this sentiment in "La muñeca negra," "Los zapaticos de rosa," and "Bebé y el señor Don Pomposo" with great agility. Nevertheless, pity stems from a fundamentally asymmetrical situation. The reality of Martí's experience, of course, is based on his observations of grossly unequal situations. He grew up while slavery was still legal in Cuba and witnessed the trauma of the auction block. Certainly, he felt compassion first hand. After his trips to Mexico and Guatemala, his identification with the treatment and the history of the indigenous cultures of the Americas also provided him with innumerable examples to inspire pity and confirm guilt: "el hecho de que los conquistadores respondieran a la hospitalidad con traición, a la amabilidad con el abuso, a la paz con el exterminio" (Gallego Alfonso 104) [the fact that the conquistadors would respond to hospitality with betrayal, to friendship with abuse, to peace with extermination]. As Martí wrote in his essay on Las Casas: "En una isla donde había quinientos mil, 'vio con sus ojos' los indios que quedaban: once" (118) [On an island where there were five hundred thousand, 'he saw with his own eyes' the Indians that remained: eleven]. Thus, while his explicit arguments in the various texts included in *La edad de oro* insist repeatedly on the ontological and essential equality of all humankind, they also reveal, implicitly, the power of colonialism to propagate an unspoken and often unconscious acceptance of gender, racial, and cultural superiority.

José Martí's limited nineteenth-century understanding of anthropology, along with his belief in modernism, Darwinian evolution, and scientific progress, preempts any possibility of arguing against the Western view of linear cultural development. Certainly the predicament that Martí finds himself in substantiates the central argument of this book that movements of independence are continuously betrayed by neocolonialism, which limits the possibility of envisioning a truly contending worldview or, as Mignolo would say, the enunciation of border knowledge.

None of these observations, however, are designed to detract from either José Martí, the man or the writer. There can be no doubt that his heroism was genuine and his desire for a classless, mixed-race society sincere. His unique status emanates not only from his actions with regard to the liberation of Cuba but also from his ideas and his forms of expression: "Con este lenguaje innovador, revolucionario y luminoso, nadie había hablado antes a los niños y adolescentes" (Elizagaray 19) [No one had ever before spoken to children and adolescents in this innovative, revolutionary and bright language]. Clearly, he was a person, in many ways, ahead of his time. Yet, he was also very much caught within his particular moment of history, though determined to change it. It is little wonder that generations of Spanish-speaking children, both in Cuba and elsewhere, have been brought up reading *La edad de oro* whose stories, poems, and essays seem as vital today as they did over one hundred years ago. His own struggle, however, with the pervasive effects of colonialism should remind us all, children and adults, of the difficulties we must continually face in the battle to identify and understand our invisible assumptions and prejudices. As he himself insisted to the children who read his magazine: "hay muchas cosas que son verdad aunque no se las vea" (164) [there are many things that are true, even though you do not see them].

3

And They All Lived Unhappily Ever After
Carmen Lyra and *Cuentos de mi tía Panchita*

Carmen Lyra (or Lira), the pseudonym for María Isabel Carvajal, made a lasting impression on Costa Rican letters. She was recognized in her own time, not only for her contribution to literature both for adults and children, but also for her leadership in politics and her efforts to improve socioeconomic conditions, especially for women and children. She helped found Costa Rica's Communist Party in 1931 and was elected its General Secretary in 1943 right before it was dissolved and reconstituted as the National Vanguard Party [Vanguardia Nacional]. She was the first person in Costa Rica to write fiction attacking Yankee imperialism and decrying the conditions on the foreign-run banana plantations (*Bananas and Men* 1931), a trend followed later by such Costa Rican notables as Joaquín Gutiérrez, Fabián Dobles, and Carlos Luis Fallas. Her most immediate and long-lasting success, however, has been her collection of stories and folklore for children: *Cuentos de mi tía Panchita* (1920).

In addition to her continued recognition within her own country,[1] she was acknowledged in a 1939 article published in the United States[2] about literary research topics on Central American writers. Furthermore, by that time some of her stories had already been anthologized in a U.S. primary school Spanish text.[3] In the academic realm, she has been a popular subject for master's and *Licenciatura* theses at the University of Costa Rica, and even one doctoral dissertation (Cantillano) from the University of Arizona. During the 1970s when structuralism was the reigning critical model in Costa Rica, research was done to discover the "metacuento" or the basic story line of all her children's tales following structuralist critics like Vladimir Propp and Roland Barthes.[4] More recently another wave of theses during the 1990s has analyzed narrative voice, folkloric elements, and Lyra's political essays.[5] An English translation of her stories from *Cuentos de mi tía Panchita* came out in 2000 under the intriguing title of *The Subversive Voice of Carmen Lyra* (Horan). Unfortunately, the title promised more than the book delivered since there was very

little analysis of the stories themselves or information about the transla-
tional problems that her use of the Costa Rican vernacular presents.

Because of the long-lived success of *Cuentos de mi tía Panchita*,
Lyra continued to add stories and rearrange them up until her death.
The collection's present form, containing a total of twenty three stories,
dates from the third edition (1956) and is divided into two major sec-
tions: the first part consists of stories her aunt used to tell, all but one[6] of
which follow the fairy-tale "meta-cuento" pattern analyzed by Benedicto
Víquez Guzmán in 1976. The second section consists of folkloric fables
with talking animals in the Uncle Remus and Br'er Rabbit tradition of
North American nineteenth-century writer Joel Chandler Harris. While
the original source material for this last section is undoubtedly African,
brought over by black laborers in the eighteenth and nineteenth centuries, Lyra has clearly "nationalized" it according to a consensus of her
critics[7] as noted on the back cover of the most recent edition (2005). Yet,
by incorporating Afro-Caribbean stories and elements of indigenous
folklore[8] into mainstream Costa Rican literature, Lyra manages to link
the subaltern status of the Central American Creole of European descent
to that of the marginalized blacks and Amerindians that inhabit rural
Costa Rica.

The most notable feature of the collection is the orality of the language,
which is certainly the aspect that has landed her in the *costumbrista* lists.[9]
But Lyra is no *costumbrista* in a strict sense of the term; in fact, just the
opposite.[10] Despite her use of popular Costa Rican speech, her tales for
children are in no way little slices of life or "cuadros de costumbres" (too
many kings and queens and palaces and talking animals), and there is
no humor directed at or against the protagonists of the stories for their
uncouth behavior or limited intelligence. Instead, the humor derives from
the language used by the narrator (not just the characters) and the obvious artifice of the story construction. There is never any attempt to erase
the distance between teller and tale; in fact, this distance is exaggerated
both by narrator commentary like "me olvidaba decir" (Lyra 147) [I forgot
to say] and by the use of formulaic beginnings and endings ("había una
vez" [once upon a time]; "y me meto por un huequito y me salgo por otro
para que ustedes me cuentan otro" [an idiomatic, formulaic ending non-
existent in English]). In addition, she offers alternative endings suggesting
that maybe events did not actually happen the way she tells them ("que
quien me lo contó se equivocara" [the person who told me could have
made a mistake]). Finally, she places kings and queens and Catholic icons

in familiar Costa Rican settings: sitting on the porch, watching people go by in the street, cooking in the kitchen, and (my personal favorite) the Virgin Mary feeding her chickens in Heaven's backyard.

In Lyra's narrative for adults, as her critics have repeatedly indicated, her political and ideological concerns are clearly visible, to the point that U.S. intelligence followed her left-wing political activities for over a decade.[11] Her children's stories, however, are very different, seemingly grounded in a fairly conventional Christian morality of virtues rewarded and sins punished. The intriguing question, then, is why a political activist, vocally opposed to the interference of the Catholic Church in government, would substitute fairy godmothers with Catholic saints and icons? Despite her anti-clerical position in her political life and adult literature, the Virgin Mary, José, Saint Peter, Jesus, and Tatica Dios/Nuestro Señor Himself through divine intervention regularly come to the aid of the various heroes in her stories to reward compassion and unselfishness. It seems odd that she would have divorced her political values so completely—indeed, apparently reversed them—in her children's stories.

My contention here, of course, is that Lyra is not departing from her political convictions; instead, she is engaging in a process that translators call familiarization. She makes her stories appear innocuous,[12] home grown, and familiar by adding local elements (Costa Rican speech, settings, religious imagery) to the imported ones. One Costa Rican critic, for example, remarks:

Es interesante notar cómo, Carmen Lyra, haciendo uso de elementos extraños—príncipes, reyes y princesas—a nuestro medio, logra meter al tonto descalzo de nuestros pueblos en los palacios, como si nada, y de esa manera ingenua los niños y los viejos aceptamos el hecho como lo más natural. (Retana 9)

[It is interesting to note how Carmen Lyra, while making use of foreign elements—princes, kings and princesses—manages to place the barefoot simpleton of our villages in palaces, as easy as you please, and in this ingenuous way, the children and we old folk accept what happens as completely natural.]

What Lyra is actually doing is creating a way for Costa Ricans to see themselves in relation to others; that is, she is helping to create a national imaginary.[13] The most visible part of this national identity is the "tonto

descalzo," the poor peasant or *campesino* with whom Costa Ricans identify.[14] Even today, almost one hundred years after Lyra published her stories, Costa Rican children are still taught to identify with the national
construct of the "labriego sencillo" [simple laborer] of their national
anthem.[15] The underlying rationale, in the formulation of such a humble
national imaginary, following Martí's lead, is to turn away from the pre-
tensions of European ancestry and celebrate simplicity, lack of formal,
Eurocentrically defined culture (*el tonto* [simpleton]), and poverty (*descalzo* [barefoot]). In other words, it is a rejection of European standards
based on money and nobility as well as a social-leveling device putting
all Costa Ricans on the same footing.

While this image appears to be self-deprecating, it is actually a cultural mask, hiding underneath it an astute figure, like Lyra's Tío Conejo
and the *campesino* heroes of her fairy tales. This occult identity, the
Costa Rican behind the simple pose, functions as a defense mechanism
in response to five centuries of colonial legacy, three centuries under
Spanish political and religious domination and the last two centuries
under U.S. economic and cultural imperialism. Outwardly, Costa Ricans
play the part of the unsophisticated, "underdeveloped," ingenuous, inex-
perienced country bumpkins, but secretly, they "know" they are smarter,
more astute,[16] experienced, able to manipulate and fool colonial power,
intelligent in a covert way (with access to subaltern knowledges that the
powerful cannot see because they are blind to the colonial difference).
This secret "astucia" is tantamount to the Dominican Ciguapa's backward feet. It allows the oppressed to have their way, to get what they
want, or to have the last laugh, without being caught, without angering
the agents of established power or awakening the beast of violent colonial, imperial, or racist domination and suppression.

"Uvieta," one of Lyra's most popular stories, is a clear example of this
cultural imaginary at work, that is, the Costa Rican ability to get the better of more powerful opponents. In this case, the protagonist, an unassuming poor *campesino* by the name of Uvieta, manages to maintain
the upper hand in dealings with none other than the Devil, Death, and
God Himself. Thus, while Lyra appears to be adding familiar Catholic
icons to her stories, she actually manages to undermine the hegemony of
Catholicism by showing how an ignorant Costa Rican *campesino* thwarts
its capricious control.

As in Lyra's other fairy tales, the protagonist takes off to "rodar tierras"
[see the world; seek fortune], a solution to problems that often repeats in

her story openings. Actually, seeing the world and seeking one's fortune are not good translations of this phrase since the purpose of "rodando tierras" is not to see anything, but rather to get away, to cover ground, generally in the direction of "montaña adentro" [into the mountains]. It is helpful to remember that in Costa Rica's particular version of the conquest narrative and colonial history, the few Amerindian tribes living in this region in the sixteenth century saved themselves by escaping into the mountains. From then on, through the nineteenth century, the colonists and later the citizens of the newly formed nation began to spread out through the country opening up new farms in the mountainous rain forests. The easiest solution to a problem, including unrelenting poverty, was to seek out virgin land, clear it, and cultivate it.

Uvieta prepares himself for the journey by buying three loaves of bread, but before he can leave an old beggar knocks at his door. Uvieta gives him one of the loaves. In rapid succession an old lady beggar and a hungry child knock at the door, and Uvieta hands out all his food. As it turns out, the beggars are none other than José, María, and the child Jesus. Each offers to fulfill one wish for Uvieta in return for his generosity and compassion. His first request is for a magic sack that will fill up with anything he wants, which in his case is usually food. In the entire story, he never uses the sack to ask for wealth. He really wants nothing more after receiving his sack and must actually be prodded and cajoled into asking for anything else. Greed is clearly not one of his defects of character, which, Lyra implies, extends to all Costa Ricans. His second request, therefore, appears to be totally idiosyncratic: since his name derives from the word for grapes [uvas], he asks for a grapevine to grow at his house where anyone who climbs up to get grapes will be unable to get down until Uvieta gives his permission. In Costa Rica, since grapes do not grow locally, they must be imported. Consequently, in Lyra's day (and to a certain extent still today), grapes were considered to be an extremely expensive, exotic fruit. His request, however, is less about having the fruit itself and more about wielding power over others who want it or, in economic terms, maintaining control over valuable natural resources coveted by imperial interests.

Uvieta's third wish, which he makes only under considerable pressure so as not to insult God Himself, is to determine the hour of his own death. All of the conversation between Uvieta and his holy interlocutors takes place in the vernacular of the Costa Rican peasant with Uvieta speaking to the Virgin Mary and José as though they were his next door

Figure 3.1.   Line drawing of Uvieta with Death stuck in the tree from *El pájaro dulce encanto y otros cuentos* by Carmen Lyra, illustrated by Hugo Díaz (EDUCA, 1993). Courtesy of the illustrator's widow, Rosa María de Díaz.

neighbors. Uvieta is so happy with his grapevine "que no cabía en los calzones de la contentera" (21) [that he didn't fit in his trousers from contentment].

At this point in the story, Lyra literally turns Christian cosmology on its head. First, "Nuestro Señor" is portrayed rather capriciously. He declares that Uvieta has had enough happiness and claims in popular Costa Rican fashion "después de un gustazo, un trancazo" (22) [after extreme pleasure, a hard tug]. Ignoring the agreement to allow Uvieta to choose the hour of his death (ignoring agreements is a tendency of imperial powers), God sends "La Muerte" [Death] to fetch the *campesino*. Uvieta, not to be outdone, encourages Death to eat her fill from the grapevine that she can see through the window. Death, of course, gets stuck in the vine (see fig. 3.1) and despite all of the messengers and threats God sends down to earth, Uvieta refuses to let her go. Nobody dies for years until Uvieta finally lets Death down on the condition that she not take him.

Nuestro Señor in retaliation, an unconventionally human sentiment for the Almighty, sends the Devil for Uvieta who recognizes him through the peephole in the door and captures him in his magic sack. He then beats the Devil into dust until God promises that Uvieta will suffer no repercussions or retaliation if he will only stop abusing the Devil. Then

Lyra slips in a most unorthodox jab at Christianity: God, in her story, remakes the Devil out of the dust. The ethical and philosophical implications of such an action are tantalizing. God, in other words, creates his own enemy, much as do colonial powers everywhere. After all, what is Christian cosmology without the Devil?

Finally, God sends Death once more for Uvieta but this time advises him to go when Uvieta is sleeping and warns him, "Mirá si otra vez te dejás engañar, quedás en los petates conmigo" (24) [See here, if you let yourself be fooled again, you'll be in big trouble with me]. Death grabs Uvieta in the middle of the night and leaves him at Heaven's gate. Saint Peter, claiming that Uvieta has already caused trouble enough "que bastante le has regado los bilis a Nuestro Señor" (24), refuses to let him into Heaven. The idiomatic phrase "regar los bilis," meaning to cause anger, literally refers to the body's spilling of bile. Thus, by humanizing God's body and attributing human emotions to him, Lyra both minimizes his status and turns him into a comic figure.

Uvieta, then, goes down to hell and knocks on the door there, but the Devil takes one look at him and runs off in fright. Finally, Uvieta goes back up to Heaven to ask what he should do now, and the Virgin (who is feeding her golden chickens in Heaven's backyard), overhears him talking to Saint Peter and invites him in: "San Pedro no se atrevió a contradecir a María Santísima y Uvieta se metió muy orondo a la Gloria" (25) [Saint Peter didn't dare contradict the Virgin Mary and Uvieta entered Glory just as pretty as you please]. Thus Uvieta, despite his official subaltern position in the Christian scheme of things, manages to get everything he wants both in life as well as in death by outmaneuvering St. Peter, the Devil, and the Lord Himself.

Lyra is neither reversing nor ignoring her professed political positions. Rather, she is writing from a place that postcolonial critics, like Walter Mignolo, call "colonial difference" and experimenting with "border thinking/*gnosis*."

> The colonial difference is the space where the coloniality of power is enacted. It is also the space where the restitution of subaltern knowledge is taking place and border thinking is emerging. (Mignolo, *Local Histories* ix)

He goes on to explain:

> The colonial difference creates the conditions for dialogic situations in which a fractured enunciation is enacted from the subaltern perspective as a response to the hegemonic discourse and perspective. Thus, border thinking is more than a hybrid enunciation. It is a fractured enunciation in dialogic situations with the territorial and hegemonic cosmology (e.g., ideology, perspective). (Mignolo, *Local Histories* x)

Lyra's collection of stories for children is one such "fractured enunciation," that is, something more than the syncretic coexistence of a marginal form of knowledge or an unsuccessfully suppressed resistance to hegemony. Rather, Lyra's stories represent a "fractured" attempt of subaltern thinking to engage in a repressed dialogue with hegemony, to complement it as well as to interject it into the discourse. Lyra herself explains in her preface to *Cuentos de mi tía Panchita*:

> Mi tío Pablo, profesor de Lógica y Ética en uno de los Colegios de la ciudad, llamaba despectivamente cuenteretes y bozorola los relatos de la vieja tía [Panchita]. Quizá las personas que piensen como el tío Pablo, les den los mismos calificativos y tendrán razón, porque ello es el resultado de sus ordenadas ideas. En cuanto a mí, que jamás he logrado explicarme ninguno de los fenómenos que a cada instante ocurren en torno mío, que me quedo con la boca abierta siempre que miro abrirse una flor, guardo las mentiras de mi tía Panchita al lado de las explicaciones que sobre la formación de animales, vegetales y minerales, me han dado profesores muy graves que se creen muy sabios. (8)

> [My uncle Pablo, professor of Logic and Ethics in one of the city's high schools, pejoratively called my old aunt's tales stupid, worthless stories. Maybe the people who think like my uncle Pablo will call them the same thing, and they will be right, because their judgment comes from their ordered ideas. As for me, who have never been able to explain any of the phenomena that continually occur around me; whose mouth drops open every time I see a flower bloom; I keep my aunt Panchita's lies right beside the explanations about the formation of animals, vegetables and minerals, which very serious professors have given me, professors who believe themselves to be very wise.]

Lyra here is defending another way of knowing, indeed, another kind of knowledge. Even though she sarcastically calls her aunt's stories "lies," she refuses to subordinate this source of knowledge to the imperative discourse of logic and reason. She is careful to place this gnoseology "beside" not beneath the Western paradigm.

"El tonto de las adivinanzas" is even more clearly an example of this border thinking at work, where a country bumpkin is able to outwit a king: "el tonto . . . no era tan dejado como creían" (14) [the boy wasn't as dumb as everyone thought]. The pose of simplicity hides a local knowledge that the colonial power—the king in this case—cannot recognize. The *campesino*, thus, wins the princess at the end but refuses to marry her because he does not want to have to dress up in fancy clothes. Clearly, he is an authentic "labriego sencillo" from Costa Rica's national anthem. Consequently, the king sends him home with two mules laden with gold, which is all he wanted in the first place. This summary, of course, does not do justice to the humor of the story, but the underlying cultural construct is clear. The "ethos" of the Costa Rican cultural identity, to borrow a term from Indian postcolonial critic, Pulin Garg, is not power, but wit.

The Tío Conejo stories all follow a similar line—Tío Conejo [Uncle Rabbit] symbolizes the astute Costa Rican in the guise of the "tonto descalzo," a trickster figure who fools and manipulates bigger, stronger, and more powerful animals, whether they are enemies or friends. Sometimes, he is out for the money; sometimes he wants something for himself (e.g., to be taller); sometimes he just wants the last laugh. The best example is "Como Tío Conejo les jugó sucio a Tía Ballena y a Tío Elefante" where Tío Conejo convinces the largest animal on land, the elephant, and the largest animal in the sea, the whale, to help him pull out his calf that is caught in quicksand. He has both animals pull on opposite ends of a rope they think is tied to the calf when in reality Tío Conejo has tied one end of the rope to the elephant and the other to the whale. Once both animals realize that they are pulling on the same rope against each other, they become furious and begin to fight, which is precisely what Tio Conejo wants:

No hay para que decir que Tío Elefante y Tía Ballena se quitaron el habla y se quedaron enemigos para siempre. Y cabalmente eso era lo que Tío Conejo andaba buscando, para que no volvieran a hacer planes de gobernar ellos dos la tierra. (Lyra 124)

[It goes without saying that Uncle Elephant and Aunt Whale stopped talking to each other and remained enemies forever. And on the whole that's what Uncle Rabbit was after, so that they wouldn't make plans again for just the two of them to govern the earth.]

It is as if Lyra foresees the Cold War, or before that, World War II. What can a tiny country like Costa Rica do when the major powers decide to take over? Clearly, it follows Tío Conejo's lead and takes advantage of the fact that as long as the superpowers are busy quarreling, no one will pay much attention to what Costa Rica does.

Moreover, since Costa Rica feels victimized economically by a rampant capitalism beyond its control, the solution once again is to turn to Tío Conejo for a few well placed economic tips. What to do to make up for years of under-priced crops? Tío Conejo's answer is to work out a plan where he sells the same crop—at an irresistibly low price—to several different buyers. As each animal/buyer arrives to pick up his merchandise, he is caught and killed by the next animal/buyer who is its natural enemy, so that Tía Cucaracha [Aunt Cockroach] is eaten by Tía Gallina [Aunt Hen], who in turn is eaten by Tía Zorra [Aunt Fox], who then is eaten by Tío Coyote [Uncle Coyote], who finally is shot by the last buyer, Tío Tirador [Uncle Shooter], a rifle-toting human. Tío Conejo ends up with five times the initial price for his corn and beans, and yet the man at the end of the story leaves with his purchase feeling as though he really got a bargain. Everybody wins, except, of course, all the animals who have been eaten in between.

Sometimes the tricks backfire on the trickster, however, as in the case of "Tío Conejo y el Yurro." In this tale, Tío Tigre [Uncle Tiger] has taken up residence at the only water hole left during a drought. He either chases away the other animals that come to drink or catches and eats them. Tío Conejo concocts a plan to scare Tío Tigre away from the water hole by converting himself into an unrecognizable monster. He spreads honey all over his body and rolls around in leaves until he becomes a giant talking bush. After Tío Tigre runs off in fright, all the other animals are free to drink water again, which they do without a word of thanks to Tío Conejo. This scenario is reminiscent of attempts by Costa Rica to help her neighboring Central American countries only to be rebuffed or unacknowledged. Part of the colonial legacy makes Central Americans invisible players in the modern/colonial system not just to the major players but to each other. Thus, the expected happy ending is inverted, and Tío Conejo "se fue muy enojado" (146) [stalked off furiously].

This tendency to invert the expected happy ending appears in several of Lyra's fairy tales as well, one in particular "La flor de olivar." In this tale a blind king is told by a passing stranger that the olive tree flower will return his sight. The king sends his three sons to search for the remedy and offers his kingdom to the successful son. One by one each son ignores the pleas of a woman beggar with a crying child. Only the last son, who "era casi un niño" (84) [was almost a child], shares his food with what turns out to be, of course, the Virgin Mary and the baby Jesus. The Virgin Mother tells the boy where he can find the olive flower, and the king's youngest son finds his two older brothers to show them. The older brothers ungratefully kill the younger son and steal the olive flower to give to the king. When they bury the brother, they overlook one important detail: "Sin querer le dejaron los deditos de la mano derecha fuera de la tierra" (85) [without meaning to, they left the small fingers of the boy's right hand sticking out of the ground]. Magically, a patch of sugar cane grows up on the spot where the fingers poke out of the earth. A passing shepherd makes a flute from one of the pieces of sugar cane, but when he begins to play, the flute sings a verse that accuses the brothers of killing him. The fame of the magic flute reaches the king who plays it himself and recognizes the voice of his youngest son. Once he realizes what the older two have done, he sends them both to the dungeon and "él y la reina se quedaron inconsolables por toda la vida" (86) [he and the queen remained inconsolable for the rest of their lives].

This summary of Lyra's tale, however, is not exactly fair, since no matter how hard I try, as a North American critic, I cannot fully liberate myself from the dominant ideology that has formed me, so that even in my retelling, I reveal a certain horror at this story of fratricide and parental suffering by emphasizing certain events and omitting others. Costa Ricans, however, do not seem at all disturbed when they read this story, and this disjunction in our immediate responses is telling. Despite the fact that the tale begins "[e]n un país muy lejos de aquí" (83) [in a country very far away from here] with a king and queen, the setting still feels like Costa Rica. The king and queen feel like everyone's own mother and father. The queen makes her own bread in the kitchen, and the father sits on the porch as people walk by (do palaces even have porches?). The Costa Rican critics who have analyzed this story all emphasize the value of the justice rendered at the end of the story through the punishment of the two brothers, but this kind of justice seems offset by the suffering of the parents, who have now lost all three children. Clearly, our critical responses and our emotional reactions have derived from different cultural perspectives, that is, different ways of constructing and understanding reality. The recognition of the border thinking at play here and the trauma of Latin American history, therefore, are fundamental in understanding what is really at stake in this story.

There is a Costa Rican saying that seems to fit this situation well: "desconfíe hasta de su hermano" [mistrust even your brother]. While the archetype of brother killing brother can be traced to the biblical Cain and Abel story, the issue of mistrust would seem to have another source that can perhaps be better traced back to the conquest. This crucial moment of physical as well as "epistemic violence" (Spivak), this infliction of the "colonial wound" (Mignolo, *Local Histories*), followed by a drawn out colonial period where the Creole descendents of European colonizers suffered a parallel subordination, produced a kind of post-traumatic stress syndrome on a continental scale. The resulting paranoia, therefore, as Mexican writer Octavio Paz notes, is not unfounded. In fact, paranoia functions as a healthy survival skill, one that is passed on from generation to generation by members of a populace who have every reason to mistrust their oppressors. After independence with neo-colonialist attitudes maintaining the logic of the coloniality of power, the paranoia toward government entities remained. This mistrust, however, over time has lost the specificity of a target and has become a generalized mistrust "even of one's brother."

Such a cultural feeling implies other ideological beliefs as well. Mistrust of others indicates that there is no clear way to distinguish between "good" and "evil"—anyone could be bad, even among friends and family, and what is more, people can change from friends to enemies or vice versa. Good and bad are not ontological characteristics of human beings, but responses to outside stimuli. The possibility to have wealth or power, for example, can trigger greed as in the case of this story. What is more, the narrative of Latin American history teaches a healthy mistrust of happy endings. Even Lyra's tales that end with the traditional marriage "and they all lived happily every after" like "El Cotonudo" have an inverted Costa Rican formulaic twist: "Y fueron muy felices y tuvieron muchos hijos y yo fui y vine y no me dieron nada" (Lyra 64) [And they were very happy and had lots of children and I came and went and they didn't give me anything].

Ironically, or perhaps justifiably, the Germanic tale of "Hansel and Gretel" seems far more horrible to the Costa Rican mentality. Lyra, therefore, takes the basic story line of the witch who imprisons two children to fatten them up to eat, and softens it for her audience. Halfway through the story, Tatica Dios Himself appears to the children and tells them how to escape. Consequently, we expect the ending; there is no surprise, no interminable, suspenseful waiting. Once the children have killed the witch, they take care to bury her (an important detail in the tropics where decay rapidly sets in). Afterward, they search her house and find a roomful of gold coins. Lyra ends anticlimactically and almost as an afterthought, since we understood from God's intervention that everything would turn out all right, "Por supuesto todo les tocó a ellos" (82) [Of course, they got to keep it all].

One of Lyra's personal favorites is the tale of "La Cucarachita Mandinga," the only fable included in the first section and the only story that does not follow the fairy-tale "metacuento." Lyra admits that the source for this story is the Spanish tale of the hardworking ant ("La Hormiguita") but claims, once again, that her aunt has Americanized it or perhaps even nationalized it. Indeed, there are variations of this tale throughout the Caribbean both with an ant as well as a cockroach as the female protagonist, usually by the name of Martina.[17] The change of the name in the Costa Rican version has invited a variety of speculations about the meaning of Mandinga (the name of a West African negro group, and in Costa Rica, at the turn of the last century, a reference to an effeminate male),[18] but Lyra, herself, explains that the term in the story does not conform to any traditional dictionary definitions, but rather acquires meaning in the minds of the children, an "other" avenue of knowing that uses Spanish in such a way that educated speakers of the dominant language cannot understand it:

¿Mandinga? Ninguna de las definiciones que sobre esta palabra da el diccionario responde a la que los niños nos dábamos, sin emplear palabras, de aquel calificativo. (9)

[Mandinga? None of the definitions the dictionary gives for this word corresponds with the one we children gave ourselves, without using words, for that qualifier.]

The children's "knowing" results from a combination of sounds that do not form words ("sin emplear palabras"), that is, communication through a non-language.

Fundamentally, the underlying theme of the story would seem to be a warning against disobedience and gluttony, but Lyra's version is heavily nuanced with sexual and racial/ethnic overtones that complicate the reading. The description of La Cucarachita Mandinga clearly caricatures an attractive Black woman from the Limón area of Costa Rica, not only for her dark color and sensuous demeanor, but also for her speech that mispronounces Spanish in the fashion of the English-speaking Blacks who were brought from Jamaica to Costa Rica's Atlantic Coast: "no me luche" for *no me luce* [it does not look good on me]. La Cucarachita is a hard worker, like the national image of the "labriego sencillo," but Lyra has converted her into an erotic black coquette with loose hair ["pelo suelto"] and a shapely body ("cuadriles" [hips]). After she finds a nickel ("un cinco") on her front door stoop, she considers whether to buy rouge, earrings, or ribbons—all accessories in the beautifying process (unlike the ant in the original story who chooses between food and rouge). Finally, she selects the ribbons since she feels that they look best on her. With her colorful ribbons and her hair down (a clear sexual marker at the time), she goes to sit at the Calle de la Estación to attract a husband.

One by one, different animals approach her to propose marriage. Before she makes a decision, she asks them in obvious sexual overtones: "¿Como hacés de noche?" [How do you do at night?] The animals respond with their various animal sounds, a stock technique in oral stories for children, but all the sounds scare the little cockroach. The animal who finally wins her over is Pérez the Rat ("el Ratón Pérez"), not only for the sounds he makes at night but also for his distinguished looks. He is dressed in a top hat and suit and carries a cane (see fig. 3.2). Clearly, this is a mixed marriage (La Cucarachita seems to be climbing the social ladder), and it is celebrated in Limonense (Afro Caribbean) style with a huge party—"una gran parranda" (66).

The next day, after she has cleaned and put a huge pot of rice pudding on the fire to cook, the Cucarachita leaves to fetch water, a secular version of the original Spanish story where the ant leaves to go to Mass. While she is gone, her husband, whom she has warned not to eat any of the dessert, cannot resist the wonderful smell of the rice pudding cooking and falls into the boiling pot. Lyra's Costa Rican readers seem not at

Figure 3.2.   Line drawing of La Cucarachita Mandinga from *La flor del olivar y otros cuentos* by Carmen Lyra, illustrated by Hugo Díaz (EDUCA, 1993). Courtesy of the illustrator's widow, Rosa María de Díaz.

all disconcerted at this unhappy ending or at his horrible death (he is scalded alive). Nor do they seem shocked by the expressions of sympathy given to La Cucarachita Mandinga: a dove pulling off its wings, a queen chopping off her leg, and an old man slitting his own throat. The enunciation of border thinking in this story, however fractured, makes perfect sense to an audience on the receiving end of colonial violence.

Furthermore, echoes from the *Popol Vuh* and Mayan cosmology infiltrate this story, reflecting a totally non-Western approach to the world where everything, whether animate or inanimate, natural or man-made, has a voice; the Occidental line dividing living things from non-living things has no place here. Amidst the mourners who offer condolences are two non-living entities, a palomar (pigeon loft) that offers to cut off its "alar" [eave], and a river that offers to dry up. The recognition by the community (all of it, whether living or not) of La Cucarachita's pain indicates an interconnectedness that is alien to the individualistic thinking within Occidentalism (what Mignolo calls egology).[19] The funeral that ends the story and that does not exist in the Spanish version clearly reflects the ethnic practices of the Limón area. La Cucarachita wants the ceremony to be "bien rumboso" (71) [very lively (from the word *rumba*, a dance)] and hires musicians to follow the coffin down the street in a rhythmic parade.

In addition to serving as a fractured enunciation of border thinking, this story also serves as an example of the density of colonial power and the layered nature of subordination. While Lyra herself, as a white Costa Rican woman, suffers the subordination of the coloniality of power, she, in turn, as a Creole representative of the dominant Costa Rican ruling class subordinates the Black culture of the Atlantic Coast. At the same time that she actively lobbies for better working conditions for the Blacks on the banana plantations, she cannot prevent a subtle condescension from escaping her description of the La Cucarachita Mandinga, "la coqueta criaturilla"[20] (9) [the coquettish little creature]. This ambivalence and cultural tension is fairly typical of the era. While on the one hand, beginning with Martí at the turn of the nineteenth century, there was an egalitarian movement to treat Blacks humanely and include them in the national project, at the same time, their culture was suppressed, discounted, and devalued as "primitive" and childlike. We should remember that La Cucarachita speaks with a childlike impediment (switching the "s" sound to "ch"), part of the orality of this story that is particularly attractive to children when read aloud. Lyra seems caught in this continental tension between a paradoxical admiration for and a Eurocentric prudish condemnation of the openly erotic and sensual Afro Caribbean female in the first half of the twentieth century.

In conclusion, Lyra's work for children may be more subversive than her readers have heretofore realized. The orality of her language, her penchant for trickster characters, her inversion of the structural expectations set up by conventional fairy tales, and her clear violation of what is considered to be appropriate children's literature from a Eurocentric, psychopedagogical perspective make her tales perfect vehicles for the transmission of a different kind of knowledge, one that appears on the margins of the Western paradigm and that exists not in opposition to but along with hegemonic discourse.

The reality of her situation, however, is that she is a woman from the third world at the beginning of the twentieth century. She faces serious limitations in any attempt to speak; her gender and her ethnicity prohibit her from talking back to, much less talking with hegemony; her gender further mutes her voice within her own locality. By liberating herself from the dominant discourse, however, and claiming the gnoseology of her aunt's stories, Lyra becomes quite a cultural revolutionary. In addition, her choice to frame these stories in a collection for children is also a strategic move. By enunciating an "other" epistemology through the vehicle of children's literature, Lyra does not threaten the adults in either her own culture or that of the dominating culture. In fact, it is precisely this claim to another gnoseology that Costa Ricans intuitively recognize as familiar and claim as their own when they praise Carmen Lyra's tales for children. One of her admirers claims, for example:

> Cuentos de mi tía Panchita—por ejemplo—constituyen un repertorio de bellas lecciones morales. Pero su moralidad no es puritanismo ni rígida norma de conducta, sino alegre invención, entre rústica e ideal . . . Por limpios estos cuentos son buena comida para el paladar de los niños. (Castegnaro 15)

> [Cuentos de mi tía Panchita—for example—constitute a repertoire of beautiful moral lessons. But her morality stems from neither puritanism nor rigid behavioral norms, but rather from happy invention, between rustic and ideal . . . These clean stories are good food for a child's palette.]

How good these stories are for a "child's palette," however, is another issue and certainly a debatable one, especially since the advent of developmental psychology. Costa Ricans, however, seem not to find Lyra's stories disturbing, despite the fratricides, cruel animal deaths, and inconsolable kings and queens. Her popularity, in fact, remains unabated; educators recommend her,[21] and Cuentos de mi tía Panchita continues to be reedited, reprinted,[22] and performed in various venues.

Her Costa Rican critics assert that she captures the "sabiduría popular" [knowledge of the people] and in the sense that Mignolo uses the term knowledge as an "other" way of knowing, a subaltern epistemology, they may have a point. But her stories do more than that. Not only does she capture the ethos of Costa Rican cultural identity with all its creativity and dynamism, she interjects this ethos into the dominant discourse through the imaginations of the children. She is fully aware of this power that she attributes to her aunt.

> ¡Qué sugestiones tan intensas e inefables despertaban en nuestras imaginaciones infantiles, las palabras de sus cuentos, muchas de las cuales fueron fabricadas de un modo incomprensible para la Gramática, y que nada decían a las mentes de las personas entradas en años y en estudios! (9)

[What intense and ineffable suggestions the words of the stories, many of which were fabricated in a way that was incomprehensible to Grammar, awoke in our childish imaginations, words that didn't say anything to the minds of older learned people!]

Grammar, with a capital *G*, represents the dominant discourse of educated people who have internalized and naturalized the coloniality of power, those who accept as universal what is no more than Eurocentrism.

Western theory which has been the only theory available for univer-salisation is definitely culture specific and grounded in the Judeo-Christian and Greko-Roman assumptions about man, collectivity and the relationship . . . They may have been internalised by educated groups of people but not by the masses. . . . (Garg 57)

Garg here is referring to the Indian masses, but the point is clear. What Lyra does is level the playing field for her protagonists. Monarchs, Catholic icons, and animal characters are all transformed into various versions of the Costa Rican peasant where what counts is neither wealth nor status nor education, but ingenuity. Lyra understands, however, the limitations of her voice; it is as though she is not speaking at all ("nada decían") to those who are blind to the colonial difference. In a sense, therefore, she speaks only to the future, to children who will grow up proud of a cultural heritage that will serve to protect and insulate them from the incessant global abuse of their already bruised and battered local egos.

4
A Question of Power
Rosario Ferré and *Sonatinas*

With her first book of short stories *Papeles de Pandora* (1976), Puerto Rican writer Rosario Ferré (born 1938) was immediately recognized by feminist literary critics both in Latin America and the United States as a new voice on the scene. Shortly afterward in a decade of heightened gender sensibilities, she tried her hand at writing and (re)writing fairy tales and traditional fables for children, publishing three collections for young readers in fairly rapid succession: *El medio pollito* (1978), *La mona que le pisaron la cola* (1981), and *Los cuentos de Juan Bobo* (1981)—all of which she later collected, reorganized, and expanded into one volume titled *Sonatinas* (1989), containing twenty-three stories.

In her introduction to *Sonatinas*, Ferré provides some background into her work and reveals some of the sources for her stories. All but two are of Puerto Rican origin, she claims; she has merely transcribed them, or in her words, "plagiarized them," although she admits to adding some artistic reformulations. Only three of the stories are her own: "añadí tres cuentos de mi propia invención: 'El reloj de cuerda,' 'Arroz con leche' y 'Pico Rico Mandorico'" (14) [I added three stories of my own invention: "The Windup Watch," "Rice Pudding" and "Pico Rico Mandorico"]. Yet her account is not quite accurate, since "Pico Rico Mandorico" is a fairly close rewriting/revision of the English poem *Goblin Market* by Victorian writer Christina Rossetti (see Morrison). Only two stories in the collection have attracted much critical attention:[1] "Arroz con leche" and "Pico Rico Mandorico," presumably for their clear feminist formulations and dissimulated eroticism. Meanwhile, the rest of her stories, many of which do not fit so neatly into the feminist critiques of the 1970s and 1980s, have been largely ignored.[2]

Looking back from a postcolonial perspective at the totality of Ferré's work for children, however, a pattern of more complex and multivariable sociopolitical critique emerges (see Hintz, "La palabra"), of which gender issues occupy only a part. Early reviews[3] of her children's collections also commented on this complexity but from a negative perspective, deeming them subversive and vulgar and claiming that these stories were not really for children at all since young readers surely could not understand them. A 1988 interviewer indicates a similar view when he asks Ferré about "fábulas que dice infantiles y no lo son" (Binder 248) [fables said to be for children but are not]. Nevertheless, Ferré insists her collections are written for children and the books have been marketed as such.[4]

Certainly, in a few instances, particularly in the stories the critics have most often singled out, Ferré's central purpose would seem to be the creation of alternative roles for women and/or the subversion of patriarchy. Nevertheless, my argument in this chapter is that Ferré's narrative is concerned less about women specifically and more about differential power distributions in general, that is, the much larger issue of asymmetry that affects the poor, the old, the infirm, non-whites, children themselves, and anyone else relegated to the margins of hegemony.[5] Ferré is fully aware that her stories allude to much more than the feminist problematic alone. In her own childhood reading of fairy tales, she claims: "La lectura de los cuentos de hadas fue un camino, una forma de entender ese mundo incomprensible, desde el punto de vista del débil, del ignorado, del niño eternamente pasado por alto" (Sonatinas 10) [Reading fairy tales was a way to understand that incomprehensible world from the point of view of the weak, the ignored, the child forever shunted aside]. Her association of herself as reader with the weak, the ignored, and the child in this comment reflects her view that women's issues form part of a much larger, more complex problem.

The fundamental differences in the power equation determine more than the degree to which various peoples have or do not have access to power (political, economic, social). These inequities also determine the degree to which various cultures accrue the means to access the structures of power, that is, the extent to which the accumulated wisdom and knowledge of what might be termed a subaltern or peripheral culture can command respect, notice, and recognition within the dominant Eurocentric/Western worldview. As postcolonial critics explain, these local wisdoms and knowledges have historically been suppressed and devalued by colonialism in its drive to "develop" or "modernize" (read "control") the "other." Ferré is keenly aware that folktales can and do serve as the repositories for collective local memory and encode alternative ways of constructing and understanding the world. Specifically, her children's stories, like her adult fiction, are an effort to address what

she sees as an increasingly fragmented Puerto Rican identity and culture at risk of being lost and overwhelmed in the global scramble to imi-
tate the powerful and efface the local. Her fiction, in general, and her
children's stories specifically, reflect her "deep disillusionment" with the
world she lives in and her need, as she explains in her best-known essay
"The Writer's Kitchen," "to re-create life, to replace it with a more com-
passionate, tolerable reality" (228; Vélez's translation).

The first story in her 1989 collection, "El medio pollito" [the little half
chicken] satirizes Puerto Rico's identity problems in the guise of what
Ferré terms a tale of the marvelous. According to Ferré's own explanation, marvelous tales differ from tales of magic or fantasy in that the
marvelous element merges with an otherwise realistic context without
causing shock or surprise either to the reader or to the fictional characters. In "El medio pollito" specifically:

> El protagonista se encuentra encuadrado por un mundo solida-
> mente real: vive en una casucha de piso de tierra, es pobre, no tiene
> que comer ni con quien jugar. Pero en medio de este mundo . . . el
> hecho maravilloso irrumpe sin que nadie se sorprenda por ello: el
> niño se encuentra con una viejecita . . . que le regala medio huevo. Lo
> insólito se introduce de contrabando en el relato, y el contraste entre
> el hecho maravilloso . . . y la cotidianidad de los hechos anteriores . . .
> es precisamente lo que le confiere al relato su poder de verosimilitud.
> (*Sonatinas* 12–13)

> [The protagonist is framed by a solidly real world: he lives in a hut
> with a dirt floor, he's poor, he doesn't have anything to eat or anybody
> to play with. But in the midst of this world . . . the marvelous element
> bursts in without anyone's being surprised by it: the boy finds an old
> woman . . . who gives him half an egg. The unusual element intro-
> duces itself like contraband into the story, and the contrast between
> the marvelous . . . and the everyday reality of the previous details . . .
> is precisely what gives the story its powerful verisimilitude.]

Within this context of the marvelous, half an egg seems believable
enough; it is the half a chicken that hatches from the egg that stretches
credibility. Ferré's explanation of how her story works, however, is only
partial. The reader's willingness to accept the marvelous without surprise (what Samuel Taylor Coleridge called "the willing suspension of

disbelief") reveals how the dominant worldview/ideology/perspective manages to make what is really not normal appear normal. The result permits acceptance of the unacceptable.

Ferré humorously implies that Puerto Rico's divided and fragmented identity, emanating from its status as a territorial protectorate of the United States, is tantamount to the plight of the half chicken. That is, Puerto Ricans are neither full citizens of the United States nor citizens of a completely free and independent country. This inherently contradictory and paradoxical status ("estado libre y asociado" [free and associated state]—as opposed to free and independent), like the marvelous existence of the half chicken, appears perfectly normal. Ferré, at the time this story was written, supported Puerto Rican independence, and even though she has now shifted her position and argues for statehood,[6] the fundamental point is the same: the status quo, the half chicken, is unacceptable. Her preoccupation with identity formation in this story for children mirrors similarly fragmented depictions in her adult fiction (cf. Peris Peris), where we find, according to one of her critics, "the recurrent image of Ferré's quest for a wholeness" (Puleo 231).

The half chicken, however, represents more than a philosophical debate over political status; it is also a graphic reminder of Puerto Rico's poverty. The little boy who owns the chicken is hungry (which is why the old lady shared her egg with him in the first place). In addition, the chicken is worse than thin; it is severely lacking, to say the least. Yet, the country itself has potentially rich resources that have historically been unevenly distributed. In his pecking for food, the little half chicken finds a tiny golden nugget (a reminder of Puerto Rico's ecological assets)(see fig. 4.1). The chicken and the boy decide to take the gold nugget to the king to exchange it for food "para tratar de aliviar el hambre de la familia" (Ferré, *Sonatinas* 19) [to try to alleviate the family's hunger]. This essential contradiction, therefore, between the island's extreme wealth and its extreme poverty forms the contextual mechanism that underpins Ferré's fiction, both adult and juvenile.

On their journey to the king's palace, all obstacles, both real and marvelous, attempting to impede the progress of the little boy and the half chicken move out of their way (the river, the guards) as long as the travelers show their gold. Money definitely talks in this tale just as it does, Ferré implies, in Puerto Rican culture. Once the two protagonists give the gold to the king in exchange for his promise to provide food, the obstacles return; neither the river nor the guards will let them pass on

Figure 4.1. The half chicken with his golden nugget from *El medio pollito* by Rosario Ferré, illustrated by Enrique Martínez.

their next attempt to return to the palace. The half chicken, despite his fragmented identity, rebels in a unique turn of the tables—he drinks up the entire river, sprays some of it at the guards and euphemistically (allusive of an "up yours" off-color expression in Spanish), puts the rest under his half a tail, "se lo metió debajo de su medio rabito" (20). When the king repeatedly reneges on his promise to deliver food, as colonial powers are wont to do, the half chicken vomits up the rest of the river and drowns the greedy monarch.

The river (a metaphor for the language of empire) is part of the dominant geology/ideology, but the water/language in the mouth of the colonized/half chicken becomes a weapon to undermine hegemony. The rebellion, therefore, turns the king's power against itself, a common strategy of oppressed peoples. The half chicken, by absorbing the water from the river and spewing it out against the guards and the king, literally inverts the river's power and converts it into a tool for liberation. Once the water returns to its bed, "repartieron muy contentos todos los bienes del rey entre los pobres" (21) [they very happily divided up all of the king's belongings amongst the poor]. Hegemony is turned upside down and good triumphs over evil in the happy world of children's fiction.

Similarly, another story in the section of marvelous tales, Ferré's version of "El sombrero mágico" [the magic hat], likewise encodes a critique of autocracy and colonial power. In fact, this story is an allegory of the power struggle and epistemic violence enacted by colonialism's hegemonic attempt to control the "other" by suppressing and erasing local knowledge and traditions. Pedro's straw hat, a gift from his mother, is the physical representation of his economic status and cultural identity "un muchacho hijo de campesinos" (39) [the son of farmers]. The king's demand that all hats be removed in his presence voices the formality that both encodes and enacts the imperial strategy of erasing/removing what the colonial subject knows about himself, that is, his or her cultural identity and personal status. Pedro, however, cannot take off his hat without another, different hat appearing in its place. As he walks to the execution block where the king plans to have him beheaded for disobedience as an example to all who defy his authority/superiority, Pedro takes off hat after hat, each hat magically replaced by a more elegant and more expensive hat, reflecting a hierarchy of social strata and status symbols, until finally he discovers he is wearing the king's hat, that is, the crown. Like the little chicken who uses the power of the water/word to undermine the king, Pedro uses the power of local knowledge/identity symbolized by the hat both to demonstrate the diversity of hats available within the population as well as to subvert the authority and hegemony implied in the monarch's hat/crown. Even though Pedro returns the crown to the king (after all, the crown represents the king's identity, not Pedro's), the people, in the meantime, have all donned the various hats that Pedro has left behind as he marches toward his execution/elimination. Despite the king's continued insistence that all hats be removed (leaving him with his monologic crown), his subjects and soldiers refuse to obey him by simply ignoring him in an act of passive resistance that promotes their diversity, multiplicity, and plurality, whether of hats, identities, local knowledges, wisdoms, or status symbols.

Precisely because imperial power robs the colonial population of its cultural identity, the artist/writer in Latin America has been forced to play such an important historical role, not only as Fuentes claimed, to provide a voice for those who cannot speak, but to preserve that voice, that is, to inscribe it, giving value to the accumulated wisdom of a community. Certainly Ferré is aware of this function in her introduction to *Sonatinas* where she emphasizes the need to preserve Puerto Rico's rich oral tradition. She explains, for example, that when she first hears a folktale from Gela, her mother's black nanny, she is impressed with "la hermosura de la anécdota, la sabiduría humana que implicaba" (14) [the beauty of the anecdote, the human wisdom it implied] and she fears that "si Gela moría sin que nadie lo hubiese rocogido, desparecería para siempre" (14) [if Gela were to die without anyone collecting it, it would disappear forever]. Her task, then, becomes one of collecting and inscribing the stories she hears: "dándole una forma más duradera al plasmarlo sobre el papel" (14) [giving it a more durable form by setting it to paper].

This role as preserver of tradition and collective memory becomes the theme of Ferré's "El reloj de cuerda," one of her three original stories in this first section of marvelous tales,[7] in which an old-fashioned, windup wristwatch is left to languish in a box of odds and ends in a jewelry shop. Everyone wants automatic, digital watches that use the latest technology. No one any longer values the simplicity of the old watch, its ability to define the essential truth in its humble identification of every hour. The tale is told from the watch's perspective, literally from its round eye, an eye that is prevented from seeing when a sale sticker is slapped onto its face. At the end of the story, the mechanical watch is purchased by a writer, who suffers from a similar disregard and subestimation: "nadie lo quería porque se empeñaba en señalarle la verdad a los hombres con la misma sencillez que él señalaba la hora veinticuatro veces al día" (38) [nobody liked him (the writer) because he tried to show people the truth with the same simplicity that he (the watch) showed the hour twenty-four times a day]. Preserving the ability to perceive from a local perspective, that is, preserving the vision of the watch/writer "la transparencia de la mirada" (38) [the transparency of sight] is key since it is this perspective from the eye of the "other" that serves as the portal to "la sabiduría de lo vivido" (38) [lived wisdom]. Ferré is talking in this story about the race to keep up with the rapid development of the industrial world and its disregard for the traditional or local understanding and perception of time.

The second section in Ferré's *Sonatinas* is comprised of her retellings of the popular Juan Bobo stories. She, of course, is not the only Caribbean writer to collect these stories, and a study of her versions along with others will be revisited in the concluding arguments of this book. Suffice it here to say that Ferré is very much aware of the subversive role that Juan Bobo plays in Puerto Rican culture, identity, and folklore. That is, he represents the same process of colonial identity formation that we see in other Central American and Caribbean imaginaries: specifically, playing dumb to hide an astuteness that is used to boycott dominant demands. Ferré explains in her introduction to *Sonatinas* that all the stories of Juan Bobo essentially impart the same wise advice: how to live the best with the least investment of work. When working implies serving exploitative masters, its value, so highly touted by Western civilization (especially Protestantism), is severely compromised. Underneath this picaresque lesson, then, lies the real social lesson that colonized people learn everywhere. Ferré explains in her introduction, "en su listura, disimulada de bobería, se percibe casi siempre un desafío al poder constituido, en un nivel político, religioso y social" (13) [in his astuteness, masked as simplicity, one can almost always perceive a challenge to the powers that be on a political, religious, and social level]. In other words, Juan Bobo knows precisely what he is doing, just as does Uncle Rabbit and the simple folk of Carmen Lyra's tales from Costa Rica. In other words, what appears to be part of the Costa Rican national identity in Carmen Lyra or the Puerto Rican national identity in Rosario Ferré goes beyond political boundaries and geographic limits to constitute a regional consciousness, the result of a shared status as subordinate and "other" and the psychological imperatives that drive survival in the face of an historically unequal distribution of power.

The third section of *Sonatinas* is labeled "Fábulas" [fables], that is, folkloric stories of talking animals, although not all of the stories included in this part abide strictly by that definition. Ferré states in an interview that she is particularly partial to this fictional genre because of its symbolic language and picaresque humor: "una cosa sucinta, directa, que tiene mucha sabiduría popular y que tiene, yo creo, mucho que ver con la manera de ser del antiguo Puerto Rico" (Binder 249) [a succinct and direct expression that contains much popular wisdom and that has,

I believe, a great deal to do with the way of being in old Puerto Rico]. The themes in this last section mirror the various political concerns that were prominent in the 1970s: "una síntesis entre la independencia política, la independencia femenina y la lucha por los derechos civiles" (Toral Alemañ 54) [a synthesis of political independence, women's independence, and the struggle for civil rights]. Ferré's growing consciousness of the divided and fragmented identity of women in particular and Puerto Ricans in general that has been noted in her other work (often taking the form of doubles, twins, close friends, or polar opposites—see Dupont) also appears in these, mostly humorous, stories. The relationship of literary critic to writer, truth to fiction, the paradoxical interdependence of opposites, and the leitmotif of hunger as fundamental motivator repeat and reverberate.

"La Sapita Sabia" is a good example of how Ferré handles the essential question of difference, whether it be sexual, racial, or cultural. A little fish makes fun of a little frog because she cannot breath underwater. The offended frog goes to her mother "La Rana Grande" [the Great Frog] for an explanation: "Hija mía, no te quejes de la sabiduría de la Creación. Sólo Ella sabe por qué hace a los seres de este mundo tan distintos, cada uno a su manera" (Sonatinas 87) [My daughter, don't complain about the wisdom of Creation. Only She (creation is feminine in Spanish) knows why she makes the beings of this world so different from each other, each one in his own way]. Since nouns in Spanish have gender, Ferré can play here with sexist stereotypes. Wisdom in this story comes from the women; both the frog and Creation are feminine. The fish is male.

At the beginning of the story when the fish controls the situation, he takes pleasure in insulting the frog: "¡Pero qué fea eres!" (86) [How ugly you are] with a fat head and eyes that stick out and an ugly voice. Later, as the water in the fish's pond dwindles because of a severe drought and the fish realizes he needs the frog's help, he suddenly has a change of heart (or tactics) and his perception about her appearance swings to the other extreme: "¡Pero qué linda eres! . . . con esos ojitos tan grandes, con esa cabeza elegante y ese croar tan hermoso" (88) [But how pretty you are . . . with those little eyes so wide, with that elegant head and that beautiful croak]. Now the situation is reversed; breathing underwater is not the standard by which everyone is judged. Being able to breathe outside the water, a different attribute, is now desirable, that is, what the frog can do but the fish cannot: "¡Se te está acabando el agua y tienes miedo, porque sin agua no puedes respirar! ¡Que esto te sirva de advertencia, para que aprendas cuál es la sabiduría de la Creación!"

(89) [The water is drying up and you're afraid because without water you can't breathe! Let this be a warning to you so that you learn to respect the wisdom of Creation].

The frog finally takes pity on the fish and takes him to another pond that has more water, underlining a clear moral: both the frog and the fish (that is, men and women or the self and the other) are necessary elements of creation. The philosophical repercussions of this moral are even more interesting. Difference becomes the defining element in creation; that is, a thing/being in itself is ontologically meaningless without the existence of the other. Essence is both what one is and what one is not. Thus, differences depend upon each other not only for survival but also for their very definition.

This play on difference forms the basis of two other stories from this final section in *Sonatinas* "El gato y los tres perros" y "La verdad y sus víctimas." The first story is an authentic fable with talking animals; the second, although listed in the section of Fables, is really an allegory. Both, however, show how the different categories of truth and fiction work together and depend upon each other for their very existence. In the fable about the cat and the three dogs, the prime motivator of the action, as is so often the case in Ferré's children's stories, is hunger. The cat leaves in search of food and picks up three dogs along the way. Unable to find food, the cat, in desperation, eats grass to pacify his hunger and accidentally swallows a little frog, the onomatopoeic "coquí," who croaks all night long in the cat's gut with a shrill *coqui* sound that does not let him sleep. The coqui is the audible voice of hunger pangs.

As the four animals approach a palace where a wedding is being celebrated (again Ferré's depiction of the extremes of poverty and wealth), they each try to sneak into the kitchen in search of food. The three dogs are discovered and hurt in some fashion by the cooks or the guests who beat the first dog, dump scalding soup on the second, and cut off the last one's tail, emblematic of the treatment of the marginalized members of society. All three, however, report back to the others that they have been given food that has somehow caused the injury. That is, they lie in order to impress the others. The cat goes last and manages to remain hidden. Contrary to the dogs who are big, aggressive, and good at attacking, the cat is small, astute, and able to hide and wait (almost invisible), eating his fill unnoticed as the food passes by. When he returns, he also tells the opposite of what really happened, "¡Ay amigos, qué mala suerte he tenido!, a mí me molieron a pedradas las espaldas pero por lo menos me mataron el coquí" (78) [Oh friends, what bad luck I've had. They crushed my back throwing stones at me, but at least they killed the coquí]. The expression in Spanish to satisfy one's hunger is literally to "matar el hambre" [kill the hunger]. Thus, the play on words revolves around how the food/stones got rid of both the cat's hunger and the frog croaking in his stomach. The cat's story/lie to the dogs in effect minimizes the differences between them and keeps them all on the same side. The humor derives from the art of lying/storytelling/creating fiction that explains something real, the dogs' various injuries and the disappearance of the frog. The synthesis, therefore, of truth and fiction is the structural link between each story segment.

In the allegory of "La verdad y sus víctimas," Truth and Fiction (lies) are twin sisters who look so much alike that people cannot tell them apart. They live in a tree, Fiction flamboyantly visible in the branches and Truth timidly hidden underneath the roots. Again, hunger is the prime motivator. Truth cannot live without Fiction, who brings her water and fruit to eat. Meanwhile Fiction, like a vocal politician, begins to make speeches to the people who gather around the tree, promising a time in which "no existirían el hambre ni la necesidad" (95) [neither hunger nor necessity would exist]. The people do not care that Fiction's words seem "poco probables; estaban hartos de la verdad" (95) [hardly probable; they were fed up with the truth]. Fiction becomes so popular that she no longer feels she needs her sister Truth and, therefore, fails to feed her. After a while, Truth begins to gnaw at the roots of the tree to satisfy her hunger, and allegorically weakens the base of the tree, which in the first heavy storm falls over, crushing all of Fiction's followers. The moral is clear: neither can live without the other. Truth or Fiction alone is like the half chicken, incomplete and fragmentary. The tree synthesizes these binary opposites providing the location for the plurality of the whole.

"La mona que le pisaron la cola" combines the linguistic repetition that children so love in a story with absurd humor and an undertone of political sarcasm. The monkey with the long tail in this story, both literally and metaphorically has her tail stepped on, a Spanish figurative expression for taking advantage of or abusing someone. While the implications of this monkey's being female are clear, she represents more than female sexual oppression.[8] She is also irrevocably linked to Puerto Rico's political/economic/cultural oppression. In search of a solution, the monkey goes to a barber to have her tail trimmed, but the brute of a barber cuts the tail completely off, suggesting a kind of female castration. After a series of repetitive and interlocking encounters with various people and their possessions, the barber's razor, a boy's baskets, a burro, a little girl, a woodsman, all of which or whom in one way or another leave the monkey worse off than before—the monkey complains: "aunque ya me cortaron la colita y por eso ando tuquita, parece como si todavía la tuviera, porque todo el mundó me la anda pisando" (93) [even though they cut off my little tail so that all I have now is a little stub, it seems as if I still had it because the whole world keeps stepping on it]. The complaint is the justified lament of the marginal elements of society, in this case, Puerto Rico itself, which is continually exploited (stepped on) by the powerful economic interests of her more developed and powerful "associate," the United States. During the colonial period, the Puerto Rican monkey was at the mercy of the Spanish empire.

The chain of events that provoke the monkey to complain that she is continually being stepped on form part of a never-ending story: "¡Y colorín colorao, este cuento entró por un callejón dorao y salió por otro plateao, pero el de la monita que le pisan la cola todavía no se ha acabao!" (93) [And colorin colorao (Spanish formulaic ending for a folktale) this story entered a golden dead end and came out of another silver one, but the story of the little monkey who had her tail stepped on is still not over]. Ferré merges the traditional formulaic rhymed ending (colorín, colorado este cuento se ha acabado [colorin colorado, this story has ended]) with its opposite—this story has not ended. It may not be pushing the images too far to posit that Puerto Rico's first dead end was Spain's desire for gold ("dorao") and the second one, the United States' drive to make money (plata "plateao"/silver), both situations resulting in the never-ending stepping on Puerto Rico's tail.

The best-known story in this last section, however, is Ferré's modernized version of the Spanish fable of the industrious little ant, who in the Caribbean becomes a cockroach, "La cucarachita Martina."[9] Martina is a self-reliant, independent black woman, who suddenly comes into money (she finds a "chavito" [a U.S. penny, the currency of Puerto Rico] while sweeping). As in the original Spanish version, she carefully considers how she should spend her money, a penny's worth of sweets, a brightly colored ribbon, or talcum powder (sweet smelling makeup) that will help her attract a husband. She decides on the latter. Her deliberative reasoning as to which purchase will benefit her the most parallels her rational choice of a husband. Martina is no romantic who waits to fall in love, nor does she plan to accept just any suitor who proposes. As she sits on her colonial-style balcony in her best dress and new powder to watch her neighbors pass by, she is approached by a variety of pretenders, a cat, a dog, a rooster, and finally Pérez the Rat, all of whom propose marriage. Clearly, Martina is attractive and knows how to manipulate her femininity to attract a mate.

Her question to each of them is specific and sexually explicit, although the child reader will probably miss the double entendre, "cómo hará en nuestra noche de bodas?" (80) [how will you be/what will you do on our wedding night?]. Each of the animals explains that it will make its characteristic animal sound: the cat will mew; the dog will bark; the rooster will crow—all with a macho twist. Each animal sound ends in a little rhyme indicating that the prospective husband plans to be in charge at home, reflecting an underlying cultural patriarchy that Ferré clearly intends to subvert: the cat "MIAOUUMIAOUU! ¡Yo mando aquí y arroz con melao!" [I give the orders here and rice with molasses]; the dog "JAUJAUJAUJAU! ¡Aquí mando yo y arroz mampostiao!" [I'm in charge here and rice and beans with coconut]; the rooster "¡KOKOROKOOOO, aquí mando yooo!" [I'm the master here]. The repeated references to various rice dishes, foreshadowing the pot of boiling rice pudding that ultimately kills Martina's fiancé, indicate from the outset that these suitors plan to be in charge of every aspect of the home, including the kitchen where women have traditionally had some autonomy. Clearly, it is not the animal sound that frightens Martina as much as losing her independence and control over her own house, not to mention her implicit rejection of these suitors' styles of dominant lovemaking.

The only animal to court Martina in a way she finds acceptable is "el Ratóncito Pérez": "¡Chuí, Chuí, Chuí! ¡Así te quiero yo a ti!" [This is how I will love you]. Clearly, in Pérez's courtship, the macho boasting of the other suitors is absent. The capital letters in the animal sounds have been reduced to lower case; the title of Señor has been removed, and Pérez is always referred to in the diminutive (el Ratoncito) [the little Rat], contrary to el Señor Gato, el Señor Perro, and el Señor Gallo. Furthermore, Pérez makes his proposal overtly erotic and seductive. He claims he will speak to her "muy pasito" [very slowly] and he whispers to her "le susurró" so that the neighbors cannot hear. Finally "ni tonto ni perezoso le besó respetuosamente los dedos de la mano" (81) [neither stupid nor lazy, he respectfully kissed the fingers of her hand] (see fig. 4.2).

Figure 4.2. La Cucarachita Martina and her suitor, Pérez the Rat, from a short story by Rosario Ferré, illustrated by María Antonia Ordóñez (Ediciones Huracán, 1990).

Martina is no innocent; she has clearly already had sexual experience (she mentions her children who will be awakened by the dog's raucous lovemaking, for example). Consequently, she knows precisely what she wants and chooses Perez for his gentle approach—"me gusta como haces" [I like the way you do it], though the fact that he is a rat sets off a number of connotative associations that foreshadow Martina's eventual deception. They set the wedding for the next day. Part of Martina's preparations, in addition to cleaning her house, is to set a pot of rice pudding to boil. Ferré describes the cooking process in such meticulous detail that she practically gives us the recipe. Clearly, Martina is in charge when it comes to the kitchen. Furthermore, Ferré's consistent comparisons in her essays and critical work between writing and cooking should not be overlooked here. When Martina leaves to put on her wedding gown, Pérez, who has an overpowering sweet tooth, is drawn to the delicious smell of the pudding and, of course, falls into the pot while trying to get a closer look. When Martina returns to stir the pudding and finds her dead fiancé, she is disconsolate, but her final comment is indicative of the gender role reversal that Ferré has implied throughout: "pero quién te manda a meterte en la cocina, a husmear por donde no te importa!" (82) [but who ordered you to meddle in the kitchen, to snoop around where you have no business]. If cooking and writing are equivalent, then Ferré's story has killed the rat just as effectively as Martina's pudding. Martina removes her wedding gown, dresses in mourning, and sits in the doorway of her house with her guitar to sing and cry. The story ends with the traditional rhyme: "Ratoncito Pérez cayó en la olla,/Cucarachita Martina lo canta y lo llora" (83) [Pérez the Rat fell in the pot/ Martina the cockroach sings and cries a lot].

Like Carmen Lyra's version of this same tale, Martina embodies the spirit of the Afro Caribbean in Puerto Rico. Her skin is dark brown like the cockroach; she is sexually independent and exotic. What lies subsumed beneath the text is "the issue of interracial sexuality that has long been a taboo in public discourse and society in general" (Puleo 230) and which Ferré explicitly confronts in her adult fiction. Martina is the comic synthesis of two characters in Ferré's adult story, "Cuando las mujeres quieren a los hombres": the sexually attractive prostitute, Isabel la Negra [Isabel the Black], and the long-suffering wife/widow, Isabel Luberza. On the one hand, Isabel the prostitute, like Martina the coquette, "is forced to understand the politics of power so that she can exercise her authority and influence in order to take care of herself both physically and economically" (Puleo 230). At the same time, Martina also epitomizes the plight of Isabel Luberza, "whose superiority and authority are solely based on societal myths that define her as a widow" (Puleo 230) and that condemn her to sing and weep in a perpetual synthesis of construction and destruction.

The final story in the collection is actually a joke, one paragraph long, that subverts one of the fundamental stories of Christianity—the Annunciation—at the same time that it highlights the foundational patriarchy upon which Western civilization is based. In Ferré's version of the conversation between Mary and the (male) angel, Mary is interrupted as she sits reading a good novel. Mary, like Sor Juana and innumerable other women, is an intellectual who is commanded to give up her studies for Church and/or family: "que lo tuyo no es estudiar sino criar muchachos regordetes y saludables" (*Sonatinas* 105) [your mission is not to study but to rear chubby, healthy little boys]. Mary is prepared to accept this situation since she assumes it means that at least she will soon get married. (Ferré has slightly rearranged the traditional timeline here or as Rosa accuses the author in "El cuento envenenado" "ha alterado des-caradamente la cronología de los hechos" (*Papeles de Pandora* 239) [she has brazenly altered the chronology of events]. When the angel explains, almost embarrassed, that she will conceive without sin, Mary responds with the punch line: "y eso, ¿qué quiere decir? ¿Que me tengo que que-dar sin la soga y sin la cabra?" (105) [and what's that supposed to mean, that I'm left without the rope and the goat?—that is, without books and sex]. Ferré's early reviewers who claim that these stories are really not for children are undoubtedly right in this instance. Children will be hard pressed to see the satire or the humor of Mary's situation in this mini story in which she is destined to have a family with neither the pleasure of sex nor the "pleasure of the text" (cf. Barthes). From Ferré's vantage point, the monkey has just had her tail stepped on once more.

The close affinity that Ferré posits between women and children (both end up in limbo upon death without ever understanding how they got there) emanates from the parallel status they share as victims of a dominant, inherently patriarchal, colonial ideology, which controls, sup-presses, ignores, and relegates them to the periphery. If, as she says and some of her critics assert, Ferré writes out of anger,[10] certainly her stories for children are also written out of solidarity in an attempt to reclaim the margins. In the critical process of learning to (re)read from a feminist perspective, as some of Ferré's critics have posited her fiction requires, it might be valuable to start from the ground up, so to speak, and learn to (re)read from the perspective of children. The nuances of parody and satire may be too complex for them to grasp, but the issues of hunger, power, and injustice they can and do feel keenly.

5
The Debate Over Racism
Joaquín Gutiérrez and *Cocorí*

In January 2003, Costa Rica's vice minister of education, Wilfrido Blanco, sent a letter to regional school administrators reminding them that *Cocorí* (1947), a short novel by Joaquín Gutiérrez Mangel (1918–2000), was no longer obligatory reading for primary school because of its "aspectos discriminatorios" [discriminatory aspects].[1] The charge of racism leveled at this prize-winning[2] children's story that Costa Ricans had been reading for over half a century, touched a nerve in the largely white, Creole population of the country. The charge, however, was not new. Quince Duncan, Costa Rica's most notable Afro Caribbean writer, and philology professor Lorein Powell had denounced the underlying racist ideology in the book twenty years earlier in 1983.[3] Gutiérrez's public defense of Cocorí, a character he had called in interviews for years "mi hijo menor" [my youngest son],[4] was sharp and personal.[5] But Duncan and Powell responded by incorporating her 1985 graduate thesis into a book (1987) with an entire chapter devoted to a meticulous analysis of the pervasive racist ideology that both frames and infiltrates the novel. Despite the bad press from the 1980s, *Cocorí* was made required reading in Costa Rica's primary schools in 1994 and was incorporated the next year into the National Exams required at the end of sixth grade (Pruebas Nacionales de Segundo Ciclo).[6] In protest, two students, Lindley Dixon Powell and Epsy T. Swaby Campbell, took the Ministry of Education to court. The court's decision (1996) found no racism in *Cocorí* but recommended, in any case, that teachers engage in a critical and historical reading of the book to put any ambiguity to rest.[7]

At this point the newly formed Asociación Proyecto Caribe [Caribbean Project Association] became involved and began to work the political scene through one of its more vocal legislators, Congresswoman Epsy Campbell[8] (mother of one of the students involved in the litigation). Ultimately in 2000, then-President Abel Pacheco worked out a compromise—he substituted the obligatory reading list for primary school with a list of suggested titles.[9] In reality, however, the compromise only created different problems. While some educators maintained that mandatory lists were bad motivators of early reading habits, others claimed that Costa Rican children would now no longer read Costa Rican authors since national authors had to compete with a number of foreign "suggestions" on the new lists.[10] The controversy had been mostly limited to experts in the field, however, until the vice minister sent out his infamous letter setting off a wave of vitriolic newspaper articles and editorials,[11] public forums,[12] and debates. The public was enraged and offended and seemed to take the charge against *Cocorí* as a personal insult.

Politics aside, *Cocorí's* unflagging international popularity is undeniable. It has been translated into ten different languages, studied in master's and Licenciatura theses (Araujo et al.; Powell), adapted for puppet shows both in Latin America and Europe,[13] and reprinted and reedited consistently over the years.[14] With each new printing or edition has come another round of favorable reviews and commentaries,[15] and apart from all the public brouhaha, scholars take the book seriously and have studied it from a variety of angles and critical perspectives for more than half a century.[16] In questionnaires conducted by both scholars and Costa Rican newspaper reporters (McDonald; Rubio, "La lectura obligatoria"; Bermúdez), most of the people queried (whether black or white, adults or children) report being unaware of any racist elements in the story. They do remember being impressed by Cocorí's admirable qualities: his courage, intellectual curiosity, determination, astuteness, and kindness.

Interestingly enough, during all of this public polemic, no one mentioned the illustrations by well-known Costa Rican cartoonist Hugo Díaz Jiménez in the 1983 edition of the book,[17] which by themselves would have been enough to support the charge of racism in the United States. His drawings are caricatures of blacks, emphasizing huge white eyes and big red lips. Cocorí's mother, Mama Drusila, looks like Aunt Jemima, overweight and with a bright red bandana tied around her head. In one drawing, with what appears to be a U.S. sailor in the background, Cocorí is carrying a watermelon, which is not even mentioned in the text (see fig. 5.1). Costa Ricans have insisted to me that that they do not share this stereotype of the watermelon-eating black; that this is a North American bias, not theirs. Still, one wonders.

As far as the charge of racism is concerned, Duncan and Powell's argument is straightforward: they insist that there are two levels of meaning in the story, one that Gutiérrez meant to tell and one that he did not, one

Figure 5.1. Cocorí holding a watermelon from *Cocorí* by Joaquín Gutiérrez, illustrated by Hugo Díaz (EDUCA, 1989). Courtesy of the illustrator's widow, Rosa María de Díaz.

about the fragility of beauty and goodness in a precarious world dominated by abiding evil, and the other, a story the dominant racist ideology tells through Gutiérrez's very choices of language and symbols (and, I would add, illustrations) without his explicit intention. The fact that the public does not consciously recognize this level, or that Gutiérrez never meant his novel to be read in these terms, does not mean that the ideological underpinnings are not there.

Clearly, Gutiérrez never meant to write a racist story[18]—he, of all people, not only one of the nation's best-known writers, but also the person chosen by a popular poll as the Costa Rican of the century in the area of literature (Martínez S.). Gutiérrez grew up in Limón, the Atlantic port area, largely populated by fourth generation blacks who were descendents of laborers brought over from Jamaica at the turn of the last century to build the railroad. According to Duncan and Meléndez, any white who grew up in Limón before 1948 (as Gutiérrez had) "es en todo sentido un limonense. Es un hombre que se adapta a la cultura de Limón. Depone sus prejuicios cliché, y se hace hermano del negro. Aporta a la cultura negra y recibe a su vez influencia negra" (146) [is in every sense a Limonense. He is a man who adapts to the culture of Limon. He puts aside his clichéd prejudices and becomes the brother of the black. He contributes to black culture and at the same time is influenced by it.].

In addition, Gutiérrez was a prominent member of the Communist Party, outspoken in his criticism of capitalism, which he maintained originated class (and race) divisions in the first place.[19] He wrote three other novels for adults with the Atlantic coastal region as the setting, *Manglar* (1947), *Puerto Limón* (1950) and *Murámonos Federico* (1973). In *Puerto Limón*, Gutiérrez was particularly sympathetic to the 1934 labor strike by the banana plantation workers that formed the backdrop for the action in the novel. The very fact that Gutiérrez chose in 1947 to make a black boy the hero of his children's novel and to give him the name of a famous indigenous chieftain[20] would seem to make him more of a revolutionary than a racist. Nevertheless, the underlying story and its racial overtones, are inescapably present. As Vásquez Vargas remarks, "Estos elementos se escapan de la intencionalidad dominante manifiesta en el libro, pero están ahí" (83) [These elements escape the dominant intentionality manifest in the book, but they are there]. Such "elements," however, were fairly standard for the time the novel was written. Caamaño Morúa, for example, describes the imagined white, homogeneous national identity of the period. She also notes, however, the contradiction of making an intelligent black boy the hero: "que un niño negro aparezca en una novela de la época descrito de tal manera, nos lleva a considerarlo un texto subversivo, que traiciona y cuestiona la ideología dominante" (930) [that a black boy should appear in a novel of the period described in this way leads us to consider it a subversive text, one that betrays and questions the dominant ideology]. Clearly, mid-century was a historical moment when Costa Rican national identity was being contested and expanded,[21] and Western civilization, with its built-in racial biases, was the only viable or acceptable model of progress and modernity.

Part of the issue here revolves around Costa Rica's cultural identity formation. Cocorí, despite his black skin, is not an outsider or the marginalized "other" in this book[22] as he would have been in early Costa Rican literature that limited protagonic figures to white Creoles from the Central Plateau. By the time Gutiérrez was writing *Cocorí*, Costa Ricans

and their literature had already opened up to a different kind of protagonist, what Quesada Soto calls "un nuevo *sujeto* social, el pueblo" (*Uno y
los otros* 84) [a new social subject, the people].

> Muchos de los textos de los autores jóvenes expresan una mayor iden-
> tificación con personajes femeninos y populares . . . los que pasan
> a ocupar papeles protagónicos y a expresar un punto de vista diso-
> nante con aspectos del discurso y la moral oligárquicos. (*Uno y los
> otros* 84)

> [Many of the texts by younger writers express an increased identifi-
> cation with feminine or popular characters . . . who go on to occupy
> protagonic roles and express points of view that oppose oligarchic
> discourse and morality.]

Gutiérrez was instrumental in adding blacks to this new social subject
that had begun to include women and *campesinos* [peasants/farmers] in
central roles. His characters are clearly drawn from the poor, marginalized descendents of Negro laborers brought from Jamaica to the Atlantic
coastal region. Paradoxically, however, despite the skin color of the characters in *Cocorí*, the story itself is not really about blacks. Alvaro Sánchez,
in his analysis of ethnicity in the national literature, notes precisely this
absence of ethnic identity: "El negrito Cocorí, el Negro Cantor y la mamá
Drusila, como fueron negros pudieron haber sido chinos sin variar la
moraleja con que cierra la obra" (217) [Little black Cocorí, the Black
Singer/Poet and mama Drusila, could just as well have been Chinese as
black without varying the moral that ends the work]. Despite the undeniable stereotypes that white Costa Ricans still have about blacks on the
Atlantic Coast, Costa Ricans fundamentally identify with Cocorí.[23] They
see him as a little seven-year-old boy, like other boys, whatever their
color: mischievous, fun loving, and astute with basically good qualities
and an amazing determination and courage for one so young. He is not
black so much as he is Costa Rican,[24] and it is this identification Costa
Ricans experience with Cocorí that I believe generated such public out-
rage at the idea that the novel might be racist. The underlying problem
with *Cocorí*, therefore, is not so much racism as it is colonialism.

Gutiérrez's choice of a rose as his central symbol with its long association in Western civilization with the theme of *carpe diem* plus his
epigraph to the novel from a Quevedo sonnet[25] indicate from the very

outset his debt to European culture. It is a debt he is proud to recognize, one that indicates that he is well read and educated by European standards. After all, the model of learning and culture at the time was European. Costa Rica, in 1947, was still culturally "primitive" in the eyes of Costa Ricans themselves. Contemporary ideas about Costa Rica's ability to inspire artistic production still largely concurred with Ricardo Fernández Guardia's notions at the turn of the century:

> Mi humilde opinión es que nuestro pueblo es sandio, sin gracia alguna, desprovisto de toda poesía y originalidad que puedan dar nacimiento siquiera a una pobre sensación artística. (qtd. in Quesada Soto, *Uno y los otros* 38)

> [My humble opinion is that our people are simple, without any grace, totally lacking any poetry or originality that could give birth to even a poor artistic sensibility.]

There is little defense of an autochthonous culture yet, and what little there is emanates from a sense of historical preservation, not from a fundamental sense of equality or from any ontological value in the local. The Rose (always capitalized in the novel), therefore, stands for everything that Costa Rica "lacks" in terms of sophistication, refinement, progress, and civilization. Thus, when the little white girl on the foreign ship gives her Rose to Cocorí, his life is changed forever. It is not until Franz Fanon publishes his groundbreaking critique *The Wretched of the Earth* in 1961 that we begin to see in this story the imposition of Western culture with its "civilizing" mission as a suppression of autochthonous cultures or to understand Cocorí's response to the rose/Rose and the little white girl as typical of the psychological brainwashing that teaches the "developing world" to devalue the local and accept as natural the "superiority" of all things Western.[26]

What Duncan and Powell point to as examples of the text's racism, therefore, on a larger scale, can be seen as the consequences of the deleterious effects of colonialism, what Walter Mignolo calls "the coloniality of power" (17), that is, the underside of modernity, the conditions, sacrifices, and costs that permit modernization to occur. With the gift of the rose/Rose, Cocorí is exposed to "civilization." What horrifies us now in the light of postcolonial criticism is Gutiérrez's indication that Cocorí is morally transformed in response to this contact; that is, he actually becomes a better person as a consequence of this gift: "el recuerdo de la Rosa endulzaba su alma y nunca Cocorí se había sentido más bueno" (*Cocorí* 22)[27] [the memory of the Rose sweetened his soul and never had Cocorí felt he was so good]. The Rose symbolically brightens its surroundings by emanating light in the darkness of Cocorí's home: "Esa noche la flor iluminó la choza de mamá Drusila" (20) [That night the flower illuminated mama Drusila's little hut]. Cocorí's intention of giving the little girl a gift in exchange, a monkey, symbol of the tropics,[28] cannot be carried out because the ship leaves. This final exchange that might have established some sense of equity or symmetry never takes place; ultimately dialogue with hegemony from a locus of equality is thwarted.

Nevertheless, there is an important initial exchange. Cocorí gives the little girl a handful of shells, "todos sus tesoros" (18) [all his treasures], symbolic of the natural beauty that his culture offers. Significantly (and unlike the Spanish conquistadors in their initial contacts with the Amerindians[29]), the little white girl does not devalue his gift. On the contrary, she runs around the ship delightedly showing everyone on board:

¡Qué lindos caracoles! Este parece un trompo, ése una estrella, aquél un pájaro—y con saltos de alegría corría a mostrarlos a todos los tripulantes. (18)

[What beautiful shells! This one looks like a top, that one a star, and that other one a bird—and jumping up and down from happiness she ran to show them to the members of the crew.]

The shells are not Cocorí's only gift to this little foreign acquaintance. He also tells her stories[30] "las mil y una historias del Pescador" (18) [the Fisherman's thousand and one stories]. Gutiérrez's clear intertextual allusion to *A Thousand and One Nights*, Scheherazade's stories, puts the Fisherman's stories on an equal footing with those from "universal/ Western"[31] culture: "Le habló del maligno don Tiburón, de las flores carnosas como frutas y de los monos turbulentos y traviesos" (18) [He told her about evil Mr. Shark, about the flowers that were as fleshy as fruit, and about the turbulent and mischievous monkeys].

The Rose, then, despite its capital letter, is not the only symbol that sheds light on its surroundings; Cocorí's stories, reminiscent of the oral tradition of the Americas, also produce light, specifically in the little girl's eyes: "A la niña se le llenaron de luz los ojos celestes" (18) [The little girl's blue eyes filled with light]. This light shines in all directions; it is not the superior light of "civilization" but rather the light of newness and difference, and it shines for both Cocorí and the little girl equally. We cannot know the ultimate effects that Cocorí's visit may have produced on the little girl since the ship leaves. The story, after all, is not about her. We do know, however, that Cocorí's effect on the little girl, in turn, makes him happy. The exchange is mutual and equal.

After Cocorí's impulsive promise to bring her a monkey, the little girl, just as impulsively, gives him a big kiss: "Ella le lanzó los brazos al cuello y le dio un sonoro beso en la mejilla" (19) [She threw her arms around his neck and gave him a loud kiss on the cheek]. What has up to this point been an intersection between cultures moves from the social level to the interpersonal. The gift of the rose/Rose is part of this exchange: "Yo también quiero regalarte algo" (19) [I also want to give you a gift]—the offer is not unilateral, but rather a response to Cocorí's generous promise to bring her a monkey. Cocorí has never seen a rose before; they do not grow wild in the tropics. His surprise and delight stem not so much from any "superiority" that the rose symbolizes,[32] but from the fact that the rose is exotic, different, and new: "Para Cocorí era algo mágico" (19) [To Cocorí it was something magical]. Thus, Gutiérrez subverts or inverts the discovery/conquest story through his rewriting of this initial gift-giving scene. As Costa Rican philologist Jorge Chen Sham notes:

Se equivocan aquellos que quieren ver, en el intercambio de presentes que escenifican los dos niños una relación asimétrica y desigual. Joaquín Gutiérrez subvierte el Cronotopo de Indias en la medida en que las nuevas relaciones entre el europeo y el blanco se presentan dentro de una retórica de la dávida, del regalo que hace encender la chispa naciente de un nuevo entendimiento. (37)

[Those who want to see an asymmetrical and unequal relationship in the exchange of gifts between the two children are mistaken. Joaquín Gutiérrez subverts the Chronotope of the Indies in that the new relations between the European and the white are presented within the rhetoric of gift giving, of the gift that sparks a new understanding.]

Clearly, Gutiérrez, in his admiration for Western culture, is blind to the colonial difference and unavoidably, however unconsciously, reinforces the notions of superiority/inferiority associated with colonizer/colonized.

As Caamaño Morúa reminds us, "El autor y su texto son producto y productores a su vez de una determinada sociedad" (31) [The author and his text are a product and at the same time producers of a determined society]. Moreover, as Rodríguez Jiménez admits, "La admiración a los rubios, concretamente a los angloamericanos, ha sido un hecho patente en nuestro medio" (58) [The admiration of the blond, concretely the Anglo-American, has been an obvious fact within our midst]. The point is, however, that despite the traces that the dominant ideology leaves within any given discourse, within language itself, Gutiérrez's text also reveals his ambivalence regarding the ultimate value of the local. That is, *Cocorí*, like literary discourse in general, is polyphonic, dialogic, and nuanced. To conclude that the text is racist or even colonialist is to adduce only a partial reading.

Part of the confusion is the result of Gutiérrez's inversion of the we/they dichotomy so that the reader identifies with Cocorí, the black boy, despite his blackness. The "other" in this story is the little white girl who arrives on the foreign ocean liner. She is most definitely not Costa Rican. Because of this inversion, the narrator and the readers never laugh at Cocorí. We laugh at his monkey, the mischievous tití, and at some of Cocorí's early antics, but once he begins his search to understand why his rose has died, our attitude toward Cocorí changes. We take his question about the rose and his consternation over a world that has become "patas arriba" [topsy turvy] seriously. His sense of loss at the departure of the ship and the death of his rose is traumatic. He literally will not eat or go out to play. We might call this today an episode of clinical depression that would worry any parent. The love and concern Mamá Drusila feels for her son is palpable. Cocorí's valient journey into the dangerous jungle in search of answers indicates his determination to discover the ontological and eschatological ramifications of his suddenly expanded world.

In addition to the we/they inversion, Gutiérrez adds another element to his story that augments the underlying ambivalence and mitigates the effects of the colonialist framework, that is, the little white girl's kiss. This spontaneous act of friendship both ignores and resists any ideological attempt to impose a binary, hierarchal structure (superior/inferior) upon the meeting of white and black. Clearly, neither child has been fully socialized yet within his or her respective ideological paradigms, and perhaps it is this partial appropriation of their separate cultural heritages that allows them to venture outside the boundaries of their individual worldviews.

To understand the ramifications of what takes place here, we need to expand upon Walter Mignolo's thesis about border thinking, that is, the local knowledge that emanates and is enunciated from that imaginary space between cultures. In addition to this concept, another should be added—that of border interaction; that is, those individual instances of egalitarian or symmetrical contact with the "other" that defy the rules of hegemony and the expectations of dominance and subordination. While the fundamental structure of colonialism and its deleterious effects on native culture and self-esteem are undeniable, individual moments, symbolized in this story by the little girl's kiss, occur from both sides—the colonizer and the colonized—that work against the dominant ideology, instances of people who meet on the border, who are transformed by their contact with the other and who can never return comfortably to their place of origin. We find such moments from the time of the conquest to today, from Bartolomé de las Casas and other monk/scholars who sensed the need to preserve indigenous culture in the only way they knew how, by inscribing it, to Rigoberta Menchú who discovers through her contact with a young Ladino community activist that not all Ladinos are evil nor can they be lumped into one denigrating stereotype.

These border interactions are the product of individuals who step outside their cultures and function in a limbo of "in between," who, whether from love, duty, generosity, or just plain curiosity, have set up residence in the psychological interspace between cultural oppositions. The overarching structure of colonialism by definition drowns out their voices and often misinterprets their actions. Yet, despite the constrictions of being socialized under different cultural conventions, a minority of individuals continues to be drawn to the border, to the in-between, by an authentic desire to know and learn from/about the "other." Both Cocorí and the little blue-eyed girl find themselves literally and metaphorically in this psychological space, on the border, symbolized here by the coast. Her kiss seals a pact of friendship between equals and functions as a sign of altruistic, disinterested love for the "other."

Clearly, Gutiérrez celebrates this contact between cultures. If not exactly on equal terms (the girl is on a huge ocean liner and Cocorí arrives in a small fishing boat) (see fig. 5.2), the two children manage to establish their own neutral zone on board where neither is superior to the other.

Figure 5.2. The big ship and the little fishing boat from *Cocorí* by Joaquín Gutiérrez, illustrated by Hugo Díaz (EDUCA, 1989). Courtesy of the illustrator's widow, Rosa María de Díaz.

Figure 5.3. The big ship and the little fishing boat from a local perspective. *Cocorí* by Joaquín Gutiérrez, illustrated by Shawn Steffler (Cormorant Books, 1989).

When contact and exchange take place on equal terms, Gutiérrez seems to say, the outcome can only be beneficial. Horizons are expanded; the local is (re)valued, not (de)valued, and the self is (re)imagined as part of a larger whole. The illustration above from the English translation of the novel exemplifies this point (see fig. 5.3). While the ship in objective measurements is larger than the fishing boat, the perspective from a position on the fishing boat makes the ship look smaller in the distance. Clearly, the local has been revalued and emphasized. Size is less important in this drawing than proximity. Through this revaluation of local identity, therefore, the possibility for symmetrical interaction emerges.

The multiple ramifications of cross-cultural contact and interaction explode in new and unforeseen ways. The problem is that this interaction is rarely carried out on an equal footing; certainly, in a colonial situation, it never is. Colonial contact presumes a one-way exchange of culture, not a cross-cultural interaction. When the local is devalued and the self is (re)imagined in the negative, then, as Duncan and Powell rightly point out, the novel falls prey to the colonialist binomials of good and bad, beautiful and ugly, big and little, powerful and weak, superior and inferior.

It is not the rose/Rose by itself, that is, the symbolic meeting of an "other" culture, that affects Cocorí so deeply, but rather the combination of rose and kiss, the meeting of an "other" human being. He recognizes the rose as a gift of friendship, not domination, and like the indigenous groups that met the conquistadors, he has offered a gift in return. It is Cocorí's contact with the other that opens up his universe, despite the initial confusions and misperceptions. The little girl's mistake in thinking that Cocorí's blackness comes from dirt is clearly part of the ingrained imagery in Western culture of white and black, beautiful and ugly, good and bad, as well as her limited understanding of the world.[33] Once her desire for human closeness takes over, her authentic yearning to know the "other,"[34] she spontaneously kisses Cocorí. It is love that motivates her gift to Cocorí, and love, not the rose, that motivates him to capture the tití to give to her as a gift in return. His sense of loss at her departure is only compounded by the death of the rose, the only part of her remaining that might have provided a clue about her "otherness." Cocorí, therefore, is left with an existential quest for love and understanding, which he tries to resolve through his incursion into the jungle.

Cocorí ventures twice into this forbidden and dangerous place, both a literal and metaphorical opposition to the safety and security of his home[35]—once to capture a monkey to give to the little girl and again later when he goes for several days in search of answers to his questions about the injustice of death: "¿Por qué mi rosa tuvo una vida tan corta? Por qué otros tienen más años que las hojas del roble?" (37) [Why did my rose have such a short life? Why are others older than the leaves on an oak tree?]. In both instances, he is accompanied by doña Modorra, the huge tortoise whose life he has saved at the outset of the novel. Doña Modorra, despite her name, which suggests drowsiness, clumsiness, and even ignorance, turns out to be a trusted friend and companion; not only does she talk in Cocorí's magically real world, but she also offers him valuable advice.

While she is not able to answer Cocorí's questions about the rose, she transmits to him fundamental information, jungle knowledge, and local wisdom. First of all, she tells him how to trap the tití: "Explota sus vicios" (24) [Exploit his vices]. Accordingly, Cocorí is able to capture the tití, not with superior strength, speed, or endurance, but with astuteness. Later, the tortoise helps him survive in the jungle by explaining to him how to determine what is safe from what is dangerous in a world where appearances deceive. She also guides him in his dealings with the crocodile, once again urging him to take advantage of the animal's vices and to escape his assault by running in a zigzag pattern instead of a straight line to take advantage of the animal's inability to gather speed in a curve. *Cocorí*, as Duncan and Powell argue, may have fallen prey to the lure of colonialist art and civilization, but clearly, Gutiérrez understands that the only way to resist the powerful is through guile. In this sense, Cocorí (like every other subaltern, including, as the late Salvadoran writer Franz Galich used to say, "el subalterno letrado" [the educated subaltern]), must learn to be astute if he is to survive in a precarious world filled with evil and treachery—whether in the form of racist stereotypes, the coloniality of power, or enraged crocodiles.

The underlying ambivalence toward Western culture in this text is evident in the lesson Cocorí learns from doña Modorra about the relativity of age and wisdom. Without an initial introduction to this dialectical view of the world, he will not be able to understand the paradox that the Negro Cantor offers by way of explanation to Cocorí at the end of the novel:[36]

> Tu Rosa vivió en algunas horas más que los centenares de años de Talamanca y don Torcuato. Porque cada minuto útil vale más que un año inútil. (78)

> [Your Rose lived in a few hours more than the hundreds of years of Talamanca and Mr. Torcuato. Because each useful minute is more valuable than a worthless year.]

Gutiérrez intentionally plays with the symbol of the rose/flower and the relativity of time when doña Modorra thanks Cocorí at the beginning of the novel for saving her life:

> Vieras de la que me has salvado, Cocorí. Si el Jaguar llega a sorprenderme en esta posición indefensa, hubiera muerto en la flor de la edad. (22)

> [Look what you have saved me from, Cocorí. If the Jaguar had surprised me in this defenseless position, I would have died in the flower of youth.]

Age, clearly, is relative, and Cocorí's rose will literally die in the "flower" of youth. To Cocorí's surprised question, "Pero . . . , ¿usted es joven?" (24) [But . . . are you young?], the tortoise explains, "Si tengo sólo ciento cincuenta años, lo que no es nada para nosotras, que vivimos tres cientos" (24) [But I'm only one hundred and fifty, which is nothing for us, who live to be three hundred]. The point is that doña Modorra speaks from the accumulated wisdom of years spent in the natural world of the Americas. Her knowledge emanates from a different source than that of Western tradition. It is neither inferior nor superior to Western knowledge, but as Martí insisted in his famous essay "Nuestra América," it is more necessary to "Americans." Western knowledge (and Gutiérrez would surely agree with Martí on this point) should only enhance local epistemologies, not replace them.

The answer to Cocorí's question about the injustice of death and the short life of the rose compared to the longevity of creatures that symbolize evil and treachery, like the crocodile and the snake,[37] ultimately comes from the Negro Cantor, the poet/philosopher, artist/singer, oracle of Greek mythology,[38] and shaman/seer from Cocorí's own community. The fact that this source of wisdom emerges from a local, rather than a Western source, highlights the fundamental ambivalence of this text.[39] Yet even he, as we have seen, is not the only source of knowledge for Cocorí. Doña Modorra, like the Negro Cantor is described as a natural philosopher: "Lo de filósofa se lo ganaba con su cara de ausente, siempre como rumiando pensamientos muy profundos" (24) [The philosopher label came from the absent look on her face, as if she were continually mulling over very deep thoughts]. As in the case of the Black Singer, other members of her community think she is just lazy: "aunque malas lenguas, como la Ardilla y la Lagartija, decían que sólo era una perezosa" (24) [although gossipers like the Squirrel and the Lizard used to say she was just lazy]. The parallels between the tortoise and the Negro Cantor are too clear to be coincidental.

Gutiérrez, like Cocorí, loves the foreign rose, but he wants to make certain that the answers Cocorí seeks do not come from colonial "knowledge" or any outside source—whether from the malevolent jungle creatures or the white foreigners. Whether human or animal, knowledge always already exists in the local and can be accessed from within through art and nature, when and if it is not destroyed, forgotten, repressed or devalued through the "epistemic violence" (Spivak) of colonial domination. Time, reflection, pause, and patience (the tortoise's attributes), are the epistemological bases for knowledge in the New World where the quicker, hyperactive, and nervous animals (the squirrel and the lizard) live hurried brief lives. Wisdom and wit prevail over other resources like speed, power, and violence (the jaguar). The squirrel and the lizard, like Cocorí's mother who calls the Negro Cantor a vagabond,[40] see only laziness in their respective community/jungle philosophers. They do not recognize the wisdom in the local creative power of survival.

The "young" tortoise teaches Cocorí the patience to grasp the extension (the time and the profundity) of life. Cocorí does not "suffer" from a clinical depression but rather "enjoys" an existential anxiety. Wisdom derives from the ability to apprehend the world, familiar and foreign. What Gutiérrez posits, therefore, are certain fundamental, transcultural (perhaps we can safely use the term universal here) verities that are common to and accessible through all epistemologies: the shortness of life, the pain of loss, the possibilities for growth.

In the end, Cocorí returns from the jungle to discover that his mother has planted the rose stem, and that it has taken root and grown into a new form: "Sus grandes rosas rojas se abrían bajo el candente sol del trópico" (81) [Its huge red roses blossomed under the ardent sun of the tropics]. The rose is assimilated into Cocorí's world, not vice versa. It must adapt to the tropics.

Cocorí has also grown and matured from his experience in the jungle. He has faced danger and overcome it: "me atreví a vencer la selva" (78) [I dared to conquer the jungle]. He has learned to value the members of his community; it is surely significant that before Cocorí goes home, he hugs both the Negro Cantor and doña Madorra, the tortoise. His brief interaction with the little white girl has, indeed, sparked a remarkable transformation in the little black boy, but not a transformation attributable solely to the coloniality of power. Rather, the story of Cocorí, despite its colonialist underpinnings, is a poignant tale of childhood love and loss, courage and understanding. Perhaps Gutiérrez's real coup is to introduce the possibility of equal and symmetrical border interaction. In so doing, he permits Cocorí to gain knowledge of the "other" that ultimately translates into knowledge of the self.

6
Dissent from Within
Manlio Argueta's *Los perros mágicos de los volcanes*

Salvadoran poet and novelist, Manlio Argueta, best known for his testimonial novel for adults, *Un día en la vida* (1980),[1] has received an unusual amount of critical attention for a Central American writer. To date he has published only two stories for children, *The Magic Dogs of the Volcanoes/Los perros mágicos de los volcanes* (1990), a bilingual edition by Children's Book Press (English translation by Stacey Ross), and *El Cipitío* (2006), also a bilingual edition (English translation by Linda Craft) published by Editorial Legado in Costa Rica. Neither story has generated much critical response yet, although *The Magic Dogs of the Volcanoes* has been included in a number of anthologies, and multicultural educators in the United States have been quick to mention it in their lists of representative works from Central America.

Indeed, Pratt and Beaty include it as their only representative of Salvadoran culture and recommend its use in a multicultural, or what they term a "transcultural,"[2] curriculum. Despite their laudable goal to open U.S. public education to a wider selection of reading material, and, in so doing, to teach children that "citizenship is extending beyond the traditional borders of individual countries to the global community" (1), their lack of basic historical information about El Salvador and Central America limits their understanding of the multiple levels and complexity of the story. Like the reviewers from *School Library Journal* quoted on the back cover of Argueta's text, they see little more than "the folklore of Central America in an attractively illustrated, accessible form." Pratt and Beaty accompany each of the works included in their study with a "Cultural Paradigm Reference Classification Chart," indicating what broad cultural parameters can be found in the text (geographic location, economic system, social system, or political system). According to their chart, Argueta's story includes only the first two categories—the geography and economy of El Salvador. The authors fail to note any information about either the political or the social system, thereby reducing the story to the themes of "antiviolence and caring for natural life in the shadow of huge volcanoes" (170). Moreover, they completely overlook the tale's sociopolitical subtexts.

The stories of the region's magic dogs, *los cadejos* as they are called in Central America, drawn from local myths and folktales, are more than mere fable and folklore. Argueta's subtexts about military oppression, land struggle, and labor issues regarding the indigenous poor are only thinly disguised. In addition, his version transforms the mythical *cadejos* (who traditionally help travelers, children, and old people) into revolutionary subjects who draw on disguise, mythology, and oral tradition to resist the tyranny of El Salvador's so-called fourteen ruling families.

Although the story is ambiguously dedicated to "los niños de El Salvador" [the children of El Salvador] (who might be expected to recognize some of the political references in the story after having lived through them), Argueta explains in his fictional biography *El siglo de o(g)ro* that the text is "dirigido a los niños salvadoreños que viven en los Estados Unidos" (211) [aimed at Salvadoran children who live in the United States]. Thus, with a bilingual edition, Argueta dramatically broadens his audience. Now, not only Salvadoran children recently displaced by the diaspora to the United States, but also monolingual English-speaking children can be exposed to the cultural heritage (and the underlying harsh political conditions) of this tiny Central American country, "nuestro mínimo país" as Argueta fondly refers to his home (*El siglo de o[g]ro* 55).

The questions are: How is this new audience to understand the story beyond its superficial level? Can Salvadoran children recognize their country's history of epic resistance to tyranny to which the tale alludes? Moreover, can the story communicate to North American children the political, even subversive, ideas that Argueta insinuates into his text when the multicultural educators, themselves, apparently miss them? The issues Argueta broaches here are internal to El Salvador, a country virtually unknown to English-speaking children and their parents in the United States. The periphery is always blurry, if not totally invisible, to the center anyway. What is the point of turning a sharp sociopolitical and economic denunciation into a mythical folktale with a happy ending? What does Argueta's story imply about his audience(s) and his relation to them? That is, who are his readers and ultimately what impact will this story have on this audience?

Salvadoran children living in the United States have already been, or soon will be, exposed to the traditional canon of children's literature, especially the Disney version, as part of their experience living in the dominant culture. Nevertheless, if they forget their own stories from their Central American heritage and oral tradition, they risk being swallowed up, incorporated, and appropriated by the growing homogenization of culture, beliefs, and values sweeping the globe. The oral tradition, if it is to be passed on under such circumstances, must be written down, indeed, inscribed. Inscription, as el Inca Garcilaso de la Vega argued over four centuries ago, is the only way to keep the folkloric oral tradition from disappearing with the advent of hegemony. Argueta has had this project clearly in mind since his work on *Un día en la vida*, that is, "el afán de llevar una historia oral a la literatura escrita" (Z. Martínez 50) [the task of transferring an oral story to written literature].

The inscription of orality also serves another and more meaningful purpose of representing peripheral groups more authentically to the official culture makers, albeit in the guise of myth and symbol. As Argueta himself explains, "el pueblo *es* su lenguaje . . . una forma de reivindicar al pueblo es dejarlo que hable con su propia voz" (Martínez 49; italics in the original) [the people *are* their language . . . One way to vindicate the people is to let them speak with their own voice]. This double goal of inscribing oral tradition for future generations of Salvadoran children and at the same time insinuating the plight of Salvadoran oppression into the consciousness of a North American audience through English-speaking parents reading to their children is paramount in Argueta's narrative of the *cadejos*.

On the one hand, Argueta describes almost poetically[3] the beauty of the Salvadoran countryside, the volcanoes Tecapa and Chaparrastique, the flowers that cover them, and the people who live there, to children who most certainly will otherwise forget, and on the other hand, he offers up a political allegory of the struggle of the people against the traditional powerful families who run the country, own the land, exploit the peasantry, and command the army. Folktales of the *cadejo*, strange wolf-like dogs who magically protect travelers or children "del peligro y de la desgracia" (*The Magic Dogs* 6) [from danger and misfortune] become in this version the object of the wrath of don Tonio and his thirteen brothers (the so-called fourteen families) who blame the *cadejos* for instigating rebellion among the peasantry. Only a magical explanation suffices to explain how the *campesinos* can turn a weakness (servitude) into a strength (refusing to serve). The strength of the peasantry, after all, resides not in the active possession of power, but in the capacity to work.

The oligarchy of the story, however, assumes that this capacity is part of the essential and ontological character of the *campesino*, something he or she cannot change or deny without some kind of magical or extraneous interference—in the story, the *cadejos* stir up the people; in the historical referent, the guerrillas, i.e., political subversives, supposedly cause all of the nation's problems:

> Los cadejos hechizan a la gente y la hacen perezosa! . . . La gente ya no quiere trabajar duro para nosotros. Quieren comer cuando tienen hambre. Quieren beber cuando tienen sed. Quieren descansar bajo la sombra de un árbol cuando arde el sol. Y todo esto por los cadejos! (*The Magic Dogs* 12)

> [The cadejos bewitch the people and make them lazy! . . . The people don't work hard for us anymore. They want to eat when they are hungry and drink water when they are thirsty and rest in the shade when the sun is hot. And it's all because of the cadejos.]

Children from El Salvador, as well as children from other cultures, can identify with the irony and injustice of this complaint, since as "children," they also live in a situation of relative oppression.[4] Like the peasantry of the story, they experience the same lack of power and control over basic resources to attend to their fundamental needs: hunger, thirst, fatigue (see fig. 6.1). Like the *campesino* of the story, the child must also follow a regime for when, how often, and what to eat, drink, and rest that is established by adults and that is not necessarily congruent with the child's own needs.

Clearly, the ruling families/government assume that the peasantry would be incapable of recognizing, much less responding, to its exploitation if it were not for the meddling of the *cadejos*, the symbolic communist guerrillas whom the Salvadoran army despises, hunts down, and tries to eliminate (with the help of U.S. president Ronald Reagan in the 1980s). The lead soldiers, "los soldados de plomo," are the toys of don Tonio and his brothers, who send them to the volcanoes to "cazar [hunt] cadejos." Argueta parodies the superficiality and vanity of the army by turning the toy soldiers into caricatures of themselves:

> Los soldados se pusieron en camino con sus tiendas de campana, sus cantimploras y sus armas centellantes.—Vamos a ser los soldados de

Figure 6.1. The magic dogs keeping a watchful eye on the peasant workers under the hot sun. From *Magic Dogs of the Volcanoes/Los perros mágicos de los volcanes* © 1990 by Elly Simmons. Reprinted with permission of the publisher, Children's Book Press, San Francisco, CA, www.childrensbookpress.org.

plomo más bellos y más respetados del mundo—se dijeron. Vestiremos uniformes con charreteras de plata, iremos a fiestas de cumpleaños, y todo el mundo obedecerá nuestras órdenes. (*The Magic Dogs* 14–15)

[The lead soldiers set out with their tents and their canteens and their shining guns. "We will be the handsomest and most respected lead soldiers in the world," they said. We will wear uniforms covered with silver medals, and go to birthday parties, and give orders everyone will obey.]

Argueta's very use of the diminutive throughout the story "soldaditos" [little soldiers] implies not only their physical size (as toys) but also connotes the lack of importance or substance in the concept of the military itself.

The metaphor of the army as lead soldiers is a rich, nuanced literary trope, given what is known today about the nefarious effects of lead on a child's brain. Argueta plays with the irony of finding mortal danger in an apparently innocuous child's toy. Lead also makes an obvious contrast to biblical clay when the narrator remarks that these toy soldiers have hearts and brains and even feet of lead; that is, they are devoid of any sign or trace of humanity. Thus, Argueta subverts the traditional fairy tale, *El Soldadito de Plomo*, which he remembers reading as a child, by turning his toy soldiers into the Salvadoran army, while at the same time undermining the military in all its pomp and ceremony.

Furthermore, he mocks the governmental persecution of the indigenous populations in El Salvador as he undercuts the military's overtly cowardly strategy for controlling the rebel forces during the armed struggle of the eighties: "Cazaremos a los cadejos mientras duerman . . . Asi podemos tomarlos desprevenidos sin correr ningún riesgo" (*The Magic Dogs* 18) [Let's hunt the cadejos while they sleep . . . That way we can take them by surprise with no danger to us]. The *cadejos*, however, like the guerrillas themselves, fool the army by becoming invisible. The magic dogs "visten un traje de luz de día y de aire, con lo cual se hacen transparentes" (18) [put on garments of air and light that make them invisible]. The guerrillas, who are peasants for the most part anyway, dress as *campesinos*, thus, making themselves invisible by becoming indistinguishable from the very social class they aim to protect. The furious military response is to destroy the crops so that the guerrillas (and by consequence, the peasants) have no food to eat; since the *cadejos* feed off the flowers that cover the volcanoes, the soldiers "comenzaron a pisotear las campánulas y a aplastar sus semillitas" (20) [began to trample the morning glories and crush the seeds].

While the *cadejos* of Argueta's story face imminent destruction from the soldiers—"Los cadejos nunca habían corrido tanto peligro" (22) [Never had the cadejos been in such danger]—the *cadejos* of oral tradition and myth face a parallel destruction as exiled children and their parents forget their cultural roots and heritage. Much like the Mayan culture, which on the brink of extinction felt "la necesidad de dejar palabra escrita de su experiencia" (Arias, *Gestos* 2) [the need to leave written testimony of their experience], Argueta, too, intuits the need to record the oral tradition from his homeland.[5] With the war in El Salvador winding down (the only reason the metropolis had taken any notice at all of the periphery), Argueta rightly foresees that Central America and all of its symbolic cultural production will once again fade into invisibility, unless the oral heritage and the revolutionary experience are inscribed, albeit in parody, myth, or children's tale, in a text that can survive the encroachment of the globalization of culture.

The solution to the conflict in Argueta's story derives from the familial relationship between the *cadejos* and their great, great grandparents, the volcanoes, to whom they turn for help. Positing the relationship between the *cadejos* and the volcanoes in such a way emphasizes the indigenous connection to their ecology and their concept of humankind and nature as two aspects of one integral being, dependent for survival on the harmony and mutual respect among all the component elements: Mother Earth, the wisdom of the elders, the richness of flora and fauna, and the work of human beings. This parallel serves to undermine even further the position of the army, which destroys crops, land, and people in total disrespect for the beliefs of the communities from which the very soldiers in charge of exterminating the opposition have been extracted.[6] The volcanoes, anthropomorphized into a man with a hat of smoke and a women with a dress of water, make a plan to erupt: "comenzó el Chaparrastique a quitarse el sombrero de fumarolas y a soplar sobre todo su cuerpo, hasta que ni él mismo aguantaba el calor" (*The Magic Dogs* 26) [Chaparrastique took off his hat and began to fan himself until it got so hot even he couldn't stand it].

The resulting meltdown of the soldiers is carnivalesque. At first, they only feel a strange itchy sensation. Then, their feet begin to melt. Finally, in despair they sit down to cry and "se les derritían las nalgas" (28) [their bottoms began to melt]. When Tecapa shakes her dress of water, the drops falling on the soldiers of lead "chirriaban, como cuando se le echa agua a una plancha caliente" (26) [sizzle like water on a hot iron]. Such is their discomfort that they finally give up and realize their impotence: "no era possible derrotar a los cadejos" (28) [they couldn't defeat the cadejos]. They cannot complete their mission; the Salvadoran peasantry still exists as do the mythical dogs from their cultural tradition despite the official attempts to eradicate them along with the popular rebellion.

There is nothing left to do but go home and sign the peace agreements: "Y sabiendo que tenían la debilidad de estar hechos de plomo, lo mejor era cambiar de oficio y dedicarse a cosas más dignas" (28) [They saw that being made of lead was a weakness and decided to devote themselves to professions more worthy than soldiering]. The insinuation here is that the military profession, itself, is unworthy and undignified. Such a criticism is far more profound than a theme of "antiviolence." Argueta casts a serious subliminal blow to North American ideology by writing against dominant expectations and turning Reagan's Freedom Fighters upside down, exposing the irony of their name, and leaving an echo that can still be heard from President Bush's forces in Iraq. Once the army went home in El Salvador, "Don Tonio y sus hermanos huyeron a otras tierras" (30) [Don Tonio and his brothers ran away to other lands]— probably to the metropolis where they can join the forces of the new global economic order—and "los cadejos y la gente de los volcanes celebraron una gran fiesta que se convirtió en una inmensa fiesta nacional" (30) [the cadejos and the people of the villages held a big party, which was later remembered as a national holiday].

Although El Salvador's political situation has not evolved as happily as the conclusion of the story might indicate, the point, after all, is not to write a realistic narrative. On the contrary, as Lucas (219) has observed, children's literature offers the possibility of rewriting history from a more positive standpoint and of opening up the alternatives of what could have been and what could be. In fact, contemporary children's literature, according to McGillis, "allows for a greater variety in versions of history and social and cultural constructions than was available to earlier generations of children" (xxviii). Moreover, the story provides a space for the child reader to identify with the underprivileged *campesino* and to function vicariously as an active agent for social change.[7]

It is here that Argueta's story becomes profoundly relevant, not only for Salvadorans but also for Central Americans in general. The fact that Central American countries share more with each other in terms of their cultural heritage than they share in terms of their political, economic, or national realities opens the space for a different configuration of local resistances whose voices may have greater strength and volume than before. The repercussions of this voice or voices, at the same time, affect the relative marginality that Central American literature suffers.

Gayatri Spivak's thesis, that the subaltern cannot speak without changing the relations of power that define it as a subaltern,[8] ultimately assumes a static opposition between the center and the periphery. In reality, the dynamism and movement between the two imply constant changes and reconfigurations in relative power.[9] As Argueta explains, "(W)ith information technologies and the interactions of migration, the periphery and the center interconnect: even more, in literature, the periphery imposes on the center" (Milan Arias 2). Consequently, the concept of the subaltern must be understood to include a variety of levels, some groups (women and children, for example) being more "subaltern" than others.

Argueta, for example, as a third world intellectual, holds an ambiguous position both inside and outside subalternity. He himself is and is not a subaltern. The late Guatemalan writer Franz Galich, for example, called himself "un subalterno letrado" [an educated subaltern]. That is, the very education and ability to speak on some level that Central American writers possess differentiate them from the mute indigenous class they inscribe symbolically into fiction. Argueta's task as a writer is, therefore, equally ambiguous and paradoxical, to speak for and with the margins, for and with subaltern groups, while at the same time producing a new way of thinking about subalternity that could change it.

This is not a new problem for Latin American intellectuals who since the time of independence have been involved with "re-construction, everything from roads and farm fields, to, especially, the manner in which future citizens should think and express themselves" (Del Sarto, Ríos, and Trigo 16). Literature has long been recruited as a key tool in this endeavor to educate the children/subaltern groups for the purposes of statehood by constructing a national imaginary. That is, there have always been didactic and rhetorical elements infiltrating Latin American narrative, stories for children included. Thus it should be no surprise that children's literature in Central America often provides this same educational or didactic function in an attempt to form future citizens and a national identity.

The role of artists and intellectuals from the periphery, however, has begun to change surreptitiously. They can no longer justify themselves and their work as part of the national project to educate the masses or as part of the project of the left to reeducate the masses. The challenge now is to recuperate a cultural heritage on the verge of disappearing. The discourse of these writers, therefore, privileges autochthonous ideas and resists official culture through irony and parody, writing against expectations, inverting the dominant scripts, and turning the world on its head. But, how, Arturo Arias asks, can an artist or writer

> que proviene de la marginalidad de la marginalidad participar en las relaciones de poder de la producción cultural y todavía así fabricar armas que sirvan para la resistencia sin entregarse al poder dominante (él que compra o rechaza libros, él que garantiza la producción, circulación y consumo de los productos que uno fabrica ya que uno mismo carece de mercado para poder hacerlo por su cuenta)? (*Gestos* 12)

> [who comes from the margin of the margin participate in the relations of power in cultural production and still create weapons that serve the resistance without giving into the dominant power (those who buy and reject books, those who guarantee production, circulation, and consumption of the products that one creates since one lacks the market to be able to do so on one's own)?]

The logical response is that Central American writers must learn to manipulate and appropriate dominant Western discourse, but in such a way as to subvert it, exposing its weaknesses and exclusions:

> De allí que el intelectual centroamericano contemporáneo mime, hable con la lengua enrollada, con una lengua picantemente paródica, irónica, esperando el momento en que pueda colarse entre las grietas del discurso hegemónico antes de que el poder de éste último lo nombre, congelándolo en el acto. (Arias, *Gestos* 12)

> [For this reason the Central American intellectual mimics, speaks with tongue in cheek, with the piquant language of parody and irony, and waits for the moment when he can sneak into the cracks of hegemonic discourse before the power of this last names him, freezing him in the act.]

What better method of sabotage than to reinscribe the cultural heritage and revolutionary experience of El Salvador in a story for children— even better, a bilingual story for children produced for consumption in the very heart of the metropolis.

Argueta's fictionalized biography *Siglo de o(g)ro* (itself a subversion of Martí's famous and overtly didactic nineteenth-century magazine for children, *Edad de oro*) offers some insights into how Argueta remembers fiction's influence on him as a child, "tantas canciones y cuentos que impactaron mi infancia" (208) [so many songs and stories that influenced my childhood]. The traditional fairy-tale heroes and heroines that he remembers "Sherezada, Simbad, Ali Baba, Aladino, los ogros de un solo ojo, las botas de siete leguas, las brujas comedoras de niños y los gatos con botas" (208) [Scheherazade, Sinbad, Ali Baba, Aladdin, the one-eyed ogres, the magic boots, the witches that eat children, and Puss in Boots] intrigue him but do not entirely convince him: "me pregunto cómo será posible imaginar tantas cosas" (50) [I asked myself how it was possible to imagine so many things]. The oral tradition he inherits from his grandmother, however, contrasts substantively with the fairy tales he reads from the Western canon and seems to him more vital, more necessary: "La magia de los cuentos los contrastaba con los cuentos de la abuela: El Cipitillo, la Siguanaba, el Justo Juez de la Noche, El Cadejo, La Carreta Bruja, La Coyota Teodora. Estos me revelaban la irrealidad palpable y amenazante" (209) [I contrasted the magic of the stories with that of my grandmother's stories: El Cipitillo, la Siguanaba, the Fair Judge of the Night, the Cadejo, the Bewitched Cart, Teodora the Coyote. The latter revealed to me a palpable and threatening unreality]. These mythical Central American figures exist in syncretic relationship to the official canon and must be continually reinscribed if regional Latin American identities are to retain any significance in the face of the rising tide of cultural globalization. Argueta is fully aware of this function of his story when he explains in a 1992 interview "his wish to preserve these tales in the hopes of helping the children recover the mentality, the mythic world, the popular imagination, and the cultural identity of their country of origin—in short, a Salvadoran consciousness" (Craft 135).

Argueta's story for children, then, is much more nuanced and layered than it at first appears, functioning as it does as an "oppositional practice" (Certau) while it subverts from within the dominant hegemonic space of the United States, using English as a weapon against itself. Children and their parents most certainly will laugh at the melting soldiers, but not with a cathartic laughter, so much as with a critical, Bajtinian carnavalesque laughter, "que escapa el control del poder vigente . . . adquiriendo el vigor de la denuncia" (Arias, *Gestos* 19) [that escapes the control of the dominant power . . . acquiring the vigor of denunciation]. The derision that Argueta provokes in his audience (children and parents alike) is part of the reeducation process, recovering the mythical past and local culture by dismantling the dominant ideology, deconstructing hegemonic values, and substituting them with autochthonous ones. The intriguing strategy here, however, is that it is opposition from within, invisible like the *cadejos*, yet effective and ultimately influential.

The very fact that children reading this story identify with a plural hero—that is, the *cadejos*, the *campesinos*, the community—instead of the individual hero of fairy tales and traditional children's literature from the metropolis, underlines the possibility for a fundamental change in the individualistic thinking of North Americans. Sympathizing with the underdog is not new for North American readers who are taught this cultural value as part of their reader expectations. A sympathetic hero who faces overwhelming odds is a frequent narrative pattern in both adult and children's literature from the metropolis and encodes what later becomes the American Dream of success, the rise from rags to riches of the outstanding individual. In Argueta's story, however, the underdog is the entire community. No individual hero, human or "dog," is singled out to receive our readerly sympathy and admiration. Narrative action is taken together by the community at large and coordinated both with the magical world and the natural environment. This is a very different story pattern from the one with which North American children are generally familiar.

Despite this difference, children from the metropolis can still identify with the heroes of Argueta's story (in a way that adults perhaps cannot[10]) because they recognize their similar subaltern position; that is, children everywhere, as well as the *campesinos* of Argueta's story, suffer a lack of effective power, status, and agency. They can understand the wish to be protected, defended, and liberated, at least implicitly, even though they do not share the same environment, economic or political situation, nor are they, for the most part, even interested in these levels of analysis. Yet, these children will not remain members of a disadvantaged group; they will grow up, most of them into hegemony, where they may be able to effect viable changes. Consequently, this position of transitory subalternity permits the young reader to comprehend at a preconscious level the Central American situation. Argueta's intentions of speaking for one subaltern group, the peasantry, while speaking to another, children, are clear. It would seem that from this angle, Argueta hopes to influence the status quo as he works to construct a unified identity among those who are disadvantaged.

While the fight against oppression continues, the site of contention has changed. The battle now must take place *inside* the metropolis, not *against* it. Moreover, the struggle has broadened its objectives and can no longer be reduced to a war between rich and poor. Now we are facing a confrontation among competing ideologies or paradigms.[11] Children's literature, therefore, will undoubtedly play a central role. In this jockeying for position among multiple values, visions, and explanations of the world, children will become the object of adult recruiting, the pawns in a global chess game. Paradoxically, this manipulation that reduces children to objects, simultaneously and inevitably converts them into the very opposite—subjects with the power of decision. Ultimately, children will have to choose between contending and mutually exclusive ideological positions. Nevertheless, they can only choose among alternatives that are available to them, and here is where Argueta's story has its greatest impact. With the publication of a bilingual edition, the magic dogs of the volcanoes succeed in crossing the barriers of North American culture and ideology. Intentionally or as a matter of consequence, the story penetrates the centers of ideological formation legally and elegantly. Like the Trojan horse, Argueta's story disguises itself within "the folklore of Central America in an attractively illustrated, accessible form" (as the backcover text relates). In a sense, therefore, Argueta has pulled off a double coup by writing from the inside out to inscribe a history on the verge of extinction. As to how much the audiences of the metropolis might be affected in the long run by this clever method of dissent, it is impossible for anyone to predict, but clearly the vehicle for transmission has already crossed the borders.

Afterword

Argueta's second story for children, *El Cipitío*, published only recently, is already going into a second edition. Although the motivations behind the book would appear to be the same as those for *The Magic Dogs of the Volcanoes* (that is, inscribing a mythical figure from the indigenous oral tradition of the region), it is far less complex than his first tale and is ultimately a description rather than a story per se. El Cipitío is a Nahautl "forest sprite," a figure hundreds of years old who appears Peter Pan-like in the body of a five-year-old child who will never grow older. He does not allow himself to be seen by adults who cannot understand him, and he frolics in the paradise of the tropics either by himself, with his little girlfriend Tenancin, or with human children, waving at them, playing, and teasing. Even though adults from the area warn their children not to wander into the woods or down to the river alone since El Cipitío may try to scare them, Argueta assures his audience that the little "duende" [dwarf] is a good child whom other children sense is not dangerous. When they hear him whistle like a bird, they run away from the protective eyes of their parents to play with him near the river where he lives.

Clearly, El Cipitío is a figure who represents un(adult)erated purity, joy, and freedom, a perpetually tiny Adam in his own Garden of Eden joined from time to time by Tenancin, his little Eve, with one overwhelming cultural/religious difference: there is no fruit that he cannot eat (see fig. 6.2). The indigenous concept of humankind's harmony with the natural environment, that is, their oneness with the All of the cosmos, contrasts sharply with the hierarchy that Christianity imposes on the universe where man rules over the animals and the forces of nature. The central prohibition against eating from the Tree of Knowledge, one of the foundational elements of the Western/Christian worldview establishes a vertical hierarchy between entities: God, angels, man, animals, plants, land. El Cipitío's relationship with his environment and ecology, however, is horizontal. It is not only that El Cipitío's world of carefree innocence cannot be understood by adults, but also that the indigenous worldview cannot be penetrated by Western knowledge. El Cipitío's universe is the unknowable "other," a world, which after puberty (or colonization), Western adults can no longer enter or even clearly remember. Because El Cipitío enjoys the protection of the Nahuatl God Tlaloc, he cannot be harmed by the creatures of the forest with which he runs wild, nude, and unashamed, in complete harmony, eternally hidden, safe, and free. His world is the utopia to which we all aspire, but to which the indigenous community must have felt a particularly poignant lack after the Conquest.

In this sense El Cipitío has much in common with the Dominican Ciguapa in that he remains hidden, naked, vegetarian (eating only fruits and nuts from the jungle); yet playful, daring, and mischievous—sneaking into human kitchens at night to steal leftover tortillas and beans. Like the mythical Ciguapas, his existence is surmised by human adults from the footprints he leaves, the traces of the other that can never be fully erased or eradicated. Even more like the Ciguapa, he disguises those footprints by walking backwards so that anyone following him will logically go the wrong way: "A veces, usa el truco de hacer al revés las huellas de sus pasos. Así, quien lo sigue, en lugar de acercarse, se aleja, y

Figure 6.2. El Cipitío and friend in a version of the folktale retold by Manlio Argueta, illustrated by Vicky Ramos (2006). Reprinted courtesy of the publisher, Editorial Legado.

nunca podrá descubrirlo" [sometimes he uses the trick of making his footprints go backwards. That way, anyone following him, instead of getting closer to him, will go farther away, and never will be able to discover him].[12] Thus, between his protection from Tlaloc and his own ingenuity, he is able to invade the human/Western world at will, steal food and play with the children or anything else he finds, without painful or serious repercussions. The combination of his fundamental innocence, his centuries of existence, and his refusal to allow himself to be seen by those who do not understand him, evokes the same psychological plight of the indigenous community, subjugated and in danger of extinction by the white/ladino community who cannot understand this "other" whom they denigrate and marginalize precisely because "innocence" in Western logic translates to "primitive," ingenuous, and inferior. El Cipitío, therefore, appeals to the willingness of children everywhere to accept the existence of "otherness" and to embrace a world in which the multiplicity of "others" eradicates hegemony.

7
Transgressing Limits
Gioconda Belli and *El taller de las mariposas*

Gioconda Belli (born 1948), contemporary Nicaraguan poet and novelist, is internationally known for her writing for adults. Few of her critics,
however, are even aware that she published a story in Germany in 1994
written specifically for a juvenile audience: *El Taller de las Mariposas*,
published two years later in a Central American edition. The over-
sized book, 12 x 14 inches, is marked by colorful surreal illustrations
by German artist and writer Wolf Erlbruch that underline the literal
level of the text, an Aesop-like fable that purports to explain the origin
of the butterfly. An English translation by Europa Books, *The Butterfly
Workshop*, was recently published in May 2006. Of the sixty-eight critical articles on Belli's poetry and fiction listed since 1994 in the *Modern
Language Association Bibliography*, not one discusses this narrative for
children,[1] clearly symptomatic of the undervaluation of children's literature in general and the invisibility of Central American children's literature specifically. My argument here is that Belli's book for children
is just as complex and aesthetically pleasing as her writing for adults.
Furthermore, her story for children reveals the same preoccupations
that underpin her work for adults: questions of gender and patriarchy,
social justice and utopia, the role of the artist and the meaning of art.

In Belli's version of the creation myth,[2] all living things, animals and
plants are invented by the "Diseñadores de Todas las Cosas" [Designers
of All Things] who are divided into various workshops. Strict rules gov-
erning the cosmos guide the Designers and prohibit them from mixing
the animals of the Animal Realm with the flowers, fruits, and plants of
the Vegetable Realm. Odaer, a young designer and Belli's only male protagonist in her entire narrative corpus, feels the rule is too limiting and
longs to experiment with his designs unfettered by the restrictions of the
Older Designers. He and a group of like-minded young designers meet
secretly to discuss all the things they could invent if the rules were different or more liberal. Specifically, Odaer wants to mix the beauty of a

flower with that of a bird, a combination that would be strictly prohib-
ited under the current system. The maximum authority in Belli's cosmology, "La Anciana Encargada de la Sabiduría" [the Ancient Woman in
Charge of Knowledge], fears Odaer's ideas will undermine the harmony
of the universe and, consequently, assigns him and his friends to a lowly
position in the Insect Workshop where they are not likely to cause any
trouble. Thus, Odaer's artistic challenge becomes how to make an insect
beautiful; that is, how to achieve his goal of artistic perfection without
contradicting the system or breaking the rules of creation. The key lies
in Belli's faith in the human imagination, for despite Odaer's position as
a Designer in the cosmos, he has more in common with humanity than
with the Gods; certainly he experiences all the hopes and frustrations
that the human condition entails. As one of her critics points out:

> Gioconda Belli plantea que la esperanza debe venir de la imaginación.
> Mientras no se pierda la fe en la capacidad de imaginar mundos dife-
> rentes, va a poder existir el mundo de la utopia. (López Astudillo 107)

> [Gioconda Belli proposes the idea that hope should come from the
> imagination. As long as faith is not lost in the capacity to imagine dif-
> ferent worlds, utopia will be able to exist.]

Some of Odaer's designs are disastrous and create monsters that frighten
even him; others produce beautiful insects that please the other young
designers, even though Odaer, himself, remains dissatisfied. Remembering
the example of his grandfather, who designed the rainbow, Odaer insists
on searching for an idealized, utopian beauty. He wants to design an insect
that is as sublime as a bird and a flower in combination. The others in his
group give up trying to reach Odaer's standards of perfection, and he is
left by himself to brood—the classic image of the Romantic, revolutionary, solitary artist. Even a dog he meets encourages him to be content with
the status quo, but Odaer is undeterred. Finally, as he sits pensively beside
a pond, he sees the shadow of a hummingbird reflected on the surface of
the water, mirroring the reds and blues of the sunset. In an epiphany, he
realizes he has found his design for the butterfly, like the perfect poem that
harmonizes with its environment in infinite variations and forms.

Odaer and his friends believe that this new creation is so important
that it deserves a workshop of its own, dedicated only to the design of
butterflies. To merit a new workshop in Belli's mythological universe,

Odaer and his friends must convince the other Designers of All Things of the significance and potential of the new design. The young Designers, therefore, work in secret to create enough varieties of butterflies to surprise and dazzle the traditional Designers. In addition, they distract the older Designers of insects by inventing the pesky fly, which they intentionally set loose by the hundreds in the main workroom of the Insect Workshop. The older Designers are so busy ridding themselves of the intrusive flies that they have no time to pay attention to the unconventional work going on elsewhere.

After five days of secret labor, Odaer visits the Ancient Woman in Charge of Knowledge to request an audience to present his new design. Although she is surprised, since she has heard nothing of the project, Odaer convinces her that all the rules of creation have been duly observed. Accordingly, she convokes an audience composed of all the other Designers (a parade of individuals who look amazingly like their designs) to view the new creation from Odaer's group and make a final decision. Needless to say, once Odaer's creation is revealed, the Designers of All Things are so impressed that they grant the group a new workshop just to design butterflies. Ever since—the story ends—Odaer and his friends have designed hundreds of thousands of butterflies.

This story on its literal level is transparent enough for children anywhere to grasp—European or Latin American, German, Spanish, or English-speaking. Belli's fable, complete with a moral interwoven in the text ("El secreto estaba en no cansarse nunca de soñar") (40) [The secret was never to tire of dreaming]), clearly emphasizes Belli's belief in the primacy of the imagination, the value of pursuing a goal, the virtue of persistence, and the conviction that dreams can become realities even under adverse circumstances. While Belli emphasizes and encourages the role of imagination in the act of creation, she makes it quite clear to her children/readers that there are limits that must be respected. The laws of creation in Belli's cosmology are not arbitrary, but symbolize the limitations that we all face, whether natural or imposed, by our very human condition. The challenge for the child/artist, then, is to create within certain boundaries, and the ultimate value lies in the attempt even when the final product may be virtually impossible:

> . . . el poder de lo utópico se encuentra precisamente en la expresión de su deseo y en su activa búsqueda aun cuando se esté consciente de la imposibilidad de su materialización. (Moyano 22)[3]

[The power of utopia is found precisely in the expression of its desire and the active search for it even when one is conscious of the impossibility of its materialization.]

Less visible or audible, especially to her child readers, are Belli's multiple subtexts that merge to form a polyphonic discourse. These partially erased narratives hidden in the form of a palimpsest, address some of Belli's ongoing concerns—political, theological, sociological, and artistic. The narrator's insistent probing of the childlike question: Why?—(Why can't I do that?)—voices the basic question at the heart of all change, invention, paradigmatic shift, or new vision produced by the frustrating imposition of limits. It is not surprising, then, that beneath Belli's literal text we can identify other texts: a story of revolutionary struggle, a reinscription of the biblical myth of creation, a deconstruction of gender and racial stereotypes, and ultimately a theory of art.

The political subtext of this story is in many ways autobiographical (as is much of Belli's work) and deals with the author's own psychological and personal struggles to come to grips with her participation in the Sandinista revolution in the 1970s. As a member of an upper-class family in Nicaragua, Belli could easily have chosen to exercise her privileged position within the status quo. Instead, her political commitment to ousting the Somoza dictatorship forced her into exile for several years. Her highly acclaimed and much studied first novel, *La mujer habitada* (1988), recounts this period of her life from both fictionalized and magically real perspectives, rewriting her participation in the urban guerrilla movement and documenting her growing dissatisfaction with the continual deferral of gender issues within the Sandinista/Marxist framework. Her second novel *Sofía de los presagios* (1990) takes these concerns even further by contemplating the situation of women in post-revolutionary Nicaragua; and her third novel: *Waslala: memorial del futuro* (1996), written simultaneously with her children's story *El taller de las mariposas*, takes the reader into the future and the possibility and loss of utopia. Belli's social and political preoccupations are no less evident in her story for children, written over a decade after the Sandinista victory in 1979 and in the wake of the political defeat of the Sandinista government to the Chamorro opposition in the elections of 1990.

Odaer and his nonconformist group are nothing less than generic rebels. They work in secret against the existing order and disagree with the limitations and restrictions that have been imposed upon them.

They have a dream and never give up, despite setbacks. Furthermore, Odaer sees his dream not in personal terms but as a goal for the general good: "Me siento responsable por hacerla más bella para los demás" (14); that is, he feels responsible for making life more beautiful for others. Ultimately, the group is successful, not because they have rebelled outright, but because they have approached their circumstances from a new perspective, synthesizing and merging apparent differences to produce a new and unique creation.

Odaer's effort to keep his dream alive, therefore, can be read as a simplified parallel to the decade's long Sandinista struggle. The existential implications of his persistence mirror the philosophy of commitment shared by Nicaragua's idealistic revolutionaries: "Si renunciamos a nuestros sueños, qué sentido tendrá nuestra existencia?" (17) [If we renounce our dreams, what meaning will our existence have?]. In other words, the story of Odaer's quest for beauty is also a story about political commitment to social change against overwhelming odds. The conclusion of Belli's story could just as well conclude the Sandinista story whose motto was "victory or death": "El secreto estaba . . . en no darse por vencido" (40) [The secret was . . . never to give up].

One has to be careful not to take the Sandinista analogy too far, however. While Belli clearly celebrates the Sandinista vision and goals, she seems to have reevaluated their methods, particularly once they seized governmental control. In fact, Belli ultimately separated herself from the Frente Sandinista, citing its authoritarian hierarchy as part of the reason and calling for a democratization of its structure to allow for the full participation of all of its leaders (López Astudillo). The story of Odaer and his friends marks this move away from the revolutionary politics of the Frente Sandinista de Liberación Nacional (FSLN) [Sandinista National Liberation Front]. Rodolfo Fernández Carballo, in his graduate thesis on Belli's novel *Waslala*, refers to *El taller de las mariposas* in his introduction as an allegory of utopia: "plantea la utopia que ha de contribuir a la belleza y la armonia del ser humano, pero sin que ella subvierta el orden existente, más aún, que tenga la aprobación de dicho orden" (25) [she posits a utopia that would contribute to the beauty and the harmony of human life, but that would not subvert the existing order; even more, a utopia that would have the approval of that order]. Politically, therefore, Belli seems more conservative in this book. At the very least, Odaer's struggle marks a change in her approach from direct conflict and confrontation to a more imaginative and consensual approach to change and creativity.

On a theological level, Belli has created an amusing alternative to the biblical version of creation. In her cosmology, Odaer, like Adam, is male; yet, the highest power, the maximum force and authority in the universe, the controller of all knowledge, is female—She who controls all knowledge. Belli's book of poems *De la Costilla de Eva* (1983) [*From Eve's Rib*] also rethinks the traditional patriarchal discourse of creation by redefining women in a positive light in opposition to the biblical tradition, which blames them for the loss of Paradise. By reversing the biblical story where Eve springs from Adam's rib, which implies that women are a derivative of male creativity, she repositions women as sources of creativity themselves. According to Kathleen March, "To see Eve as Creator does not imply a rejection or humorous dismissal of the male sex . . . but rather . . . a return to and a focussing [*sic*] upon, a matricentric world-view such as that of antiquity" (246). Sofía (whose name is clearly associated with wisdom) is a character from Belli's second novel who also offers an alternative view of women as intrinsically more in tune with the universe. Thus, Belli manages to redeem wisdom (traditionally associated with the feminine in antiquity but undermined by biblical discourse with the omniscience of a patriarchal God) as a female attribute in her children's story with "La Anciana Encargada de la Sabiduría"—the old woman in charge of wisdom.

This gender shift in our traditional patriarchal conceptions about God is merely the first and most obvious transgression against orthodoxy in this tale. The illustrations that accompany the text insinuate a host of additional subversions and transgressions far more radical and heretical.[4] First, the Ancient Woman in Charge of Knowledge is also a person of color (see fig. 7.1). Her skin is dark and her exaggerated facial features form a caricature of a native American/Amerindian. More disturbing, however, are her red dress, the serpent-like cane she carries, and her phallic index finger, which she is always pointing. This sexually ambiguous image is consistent, however, with the archetype of the Great Mother: "Mother Earth, origin of all, had both male and female attributes, her symbols such as the moon, the bull, and the serpent" (March 255).

Traditional connotations associated with race (black/indigenous), the red dress (symbol of sexual transgression), and the serpent (biblical symbol of evil) are sub(in)verted in their association with the Ancient Woman. Like God, her Christian counterpart, la Anciana has a monopoly on wisdom (the tree of knowledge) and a set of restrictions, such as the prohibition to Adam, which must be obeyed. In Belli's cosmos,

Figure 7.1. The old woman in charge of wisdom from *The Butterfly Workshop* by Gioconda Belli, illustrated by Wolf Erlbruch (1994). Reprinted courtesy of the publisher, Peter Hammer Verlag.

however, Odaer finds a way to get what he wants without direct defiance or disobedience, thus avoiding the punishment of Adam. Like the true subaltern he is, Odaer figures out how to manipulate the system.

While the symbolic sexual overtones in the illustrations clearly work to subvert patriarchal discourse, they also serve to reinforce La Anciana's authoritative stature as an ontologically complete and independent being, in charge of her own sexuality, indicating, directing, and delegating with that outstretched finger. Yet, certainly she is an unconventional authority. Unlike the visionary image that Christianity projects of omniscience, Belli's keeper of knowledge stares out from behind a pair of thick glasses, more reminiscent of Argentinean Jorge Luis Borges, the blind librarian, than a Christian God who sees every sparrow fall. Furthermore, contrary to the Christian tradition of Genesis, where God omnipotent creates the world by Himself, Belli's Ancient Woman delegates creation to the various workshops. This idea of creation as a product of teamwork fits the ideals of the early FSLN. Furthermore, the image of creation as the product of hard work and physical compromise is consistent with Belli's poetry, where she portrays God with hammer and drill in hand:

> Todo lo creó suavemente
> A martillazos de soplidos
> Y taladrazos de amor ("Y Dios me hizo mujer")

> [He created everything softly
> Hammering with puffs of air
> And drilling with love] (translation mine)

The Ancient Woman's managerial style also contradicts the patriarchal autocracy of the Church (and what turned out to be a similar structure within the Sandinista Party). Her decisions are not top-down, but consensual; when Odaer asks for a new workshop, he must convince the other Designers of All Things, not just the Ancient Woman.

Finally, a more subtle transgression: the work week is reduced to five days, rather than the biblical six with rest on the seventh day. Work is continuous and ongoing. There is no rest for dreamers. In Belli's system, even when Odaer sits by the pond, he is overwhelmed by thought and desire: "No podré descansar hasta que no pueda diseñar algo que sea tan bello como un pájaro y una flor" (13)—that is, he literally cannot rest until he designs something as beautiful as a bird and a flower. Only the dog he meets seems perfectly content to accept the status quo, "Soy feliz con sólo tener un lugar donde echarme" (13) [I'm happy just having a place to lie down]. By setting up an opposition between Odaer, our hero, and the dog, Belli makes a clear statement; only dogs give up and lie down. The dog represents everything that Belli opposes in artistic creation: "La gente que escribe no puede hacerse eco de la desesperanza, ni tampoco venderse, en el sentido de convertirse únicamente en entretenedores" (interview with López Astudillo 107) [People who write cannot become an echo of despair, nor can they sell out, in the sense of becoming mere entertainers].

Belli's Anciana is truly an ambiguous and paradoxical figure. The narrator calls her the boss—*la jefa* de los Diseñadores de Todas las Cosas. Her job, it would seem, is to maintain harmony in the universe; consequently, Odaer and his friends' insistence on thinking of all the things they could invent if the rules were different concerns her: "se preocupó y decidió que era necesario hacer algo que impidiera que las ideas de Odaer se hicieran populares, ya que ponían en peligro la armonía de la creación" (7) [she worried and decided it was necessary to do something to prevent Odaer's ideas from becoming popular, since they could endanger the harmony of creation]. From a political standpoint, this kind of justification of the status quo sounds like a tyrannical Somoza-type railing against the ideas of the FSLN. From a theological standpoint, it smacks of the rigid control of the Catholic Church. Yet, the boss is not depicted as a tyrant or an autocrat as the text progresses, and visually, she is the subversion of a conventional leader. Her gender, her color, her exaggerated Mayan nose and high cheekbones, salient racial features of the New World Indians, her obesity and poor vision, form a composite picture that resists and subverts the Eurocentric concept of beauty. She is portrayed more as a wise old grandmother figure than as a goddess. It is significant, therefore, that in one picture Odaer is sitting on her lap (see fig. 7.2).

Political and religious parallels aside, the more important issue under discussion in this story would seem to be the concept of beauty: what it is and what it does or should do. In this sense the Ancient Woman in charge of knowledge seems to have rightly come by her position. While she demotes Odaer and his group to the dusty Insect Workshop to keep them out of trouble, she argues against Odaer's conventional complaint that insects are not beautiful. "Y quién dice que no pueden serlo . . . Háganlos bellos. De ustedes depende. Tienen toda la libertad para diseñarlos como mejor les parezca" (Belli, *El taller* 7) [And who says they can't be? Make them beautiful. It depends on you. You have complete freedom to design them how ever you think best]. Although Odaer considers that the rule against mixing plants and animals is too restrictive, he paradoxically restricts his own conception of beauty by conventional ideas, conventions that the Anciana both contradicts verbally and subverts through her visual presence. Her advice to the young designer is not only aesthetic, however; it can also be read on a theological and political level as well:

Figure 7.2. Odaer sitting on the old woman's lap from *The Butterfly Workshop* by Gioconda Belli, illustrated by Wolf Erlbruch (1994). Reprinted courtesy of the publisher, Peter Hammer Verlag.

En tu búsqueda del diseño perfecto, puedes crear monstruos. Tu afán de hacer la vida más agradable y bella, puede resultar, si no eres cuidadoso, en dolor y miedo para otras creaturas de la naturaleza. (10)

[In your search for the perfect design, you can create monsters. Your urge to make life better and more beautiful, if you're not careful, can result in pain and fear for other creatures in nature.]

Belli's critique here of the Sandinista government is hardly subtle. She makes an incontrovertible distinction between a dream and an obsession. An admirable goal, she seems to say, whether political, theological, or artistic, still must carefully monitor its means: "La búsqueda de

la belleza y de la perfección está llena de tropiezos. Muchos se han perdido en el camino" (11) [The search for beauty and perfection is full
of obstacles. Many have gotten lost along the way]. Such a search, she
implies, is tantamount to the search for knowledge in Christian theology where so many with lofty goals, from Satan to Adam, have fallen.
Equally, the Anciana's remark may be read as a comment on revolu-
tions gone wrong, from France's guillotine to the Mexican Revolution's
paradón, to the infighting among the Sandinistas once they had ousted
Somoza in Nicaragua.

In addition to the political and theological nuances of Belli's story,
therefore, the underlying dialogue about the nature of beauty and art
and the role of the artist in society is at issue. Belli joins this discusion-
in-progress that begins with the pre-Columbian Amerindian cultures of
the Isthmus and reaches its zenith in Nicaragua in 1888 with the publication of Rubén Darío's *Azul*. Every Nicaraguan poet, indeed every
Central American poet after Darío, has had to come to terms in one way
or another with the impact of the indigenous past on the present and
the impact of *modernismo* on aesthetics. These concerns are not unique
to this story but represent Belli's ongoing preoccupation with the role of
artistic production within society.

> Para ella, el reto más grande de la creación es encontrar en este
> momento de la historia (cualquiera que sea) . . . cómo se puede inser-
> tar el escritor o escritora con su trabajo creativo y mantener viva la
> esperanza, incluso convertirse en un creador o creadora de posibili-
> dades. (López Astudillo 106)

> [For her, the biggest challenge in creation is to find in this historical
> moment (whatever it might be) . . . how the writer can intervene with
> his or her creative work to keep hope alive, and even to convert him-
> self or herself into a creator of possibilities.]

Odaer, when he talks to those around him, merely sets the stage for
Belli to talk back to the past, engaging in a diachronic dialogue about the
meaning of beauty and the purpose of art. At one point a rock asks Odaer
"Pero, cuál es el sentido de una flor? . . . Se marchita muy pronto y muere"
(21) [But what is the meaning of a flower? It soon wilts and dies]. It is significant that in Belli's story the rocks and the dogs talk just as they do in
the Mayan creation myth recounted in the *Popol Vuh*. The fact that the

rock asks about the meaning of a flower can be seen either as ironic, from a Western perspective, or as completely consistent with an Amerindian perspective that holds that all things, whether animate and inanimate, have a spirit or soul, and as such are all connected. In this way, Belli's magically real world of Western children's literature (where animals, plants, and rocks routinely talk and have feelings) converges with the cosmological vision of the Mayan communities where humans and the natural world are interrelated and interdependent. This notion of interconnectedness is not limited to Belli's story for children, however; literary analyses of the new ecocritical school[5] have begun to study the role of nature in Belli's other work.

Odaer's response to the rock's question is ambivalent: it both agrees and disagrees with Darío's defense of art for art's sake: "Se hace fruto . . . Pero además es bella. Lo bello no se puede explicar, se siente" (21) [It bears fruit . . . But in addition, it is beautiful. Beauty cannot be explained; one feels it]. Certainly, Darío would agree with Odaer and Belli's articulation of art as felt experience, but he might be less willing to concede that art or beauty bears fruit and that this function gives art meaning. Belli, in a recent interview, insists, however, on this functional aspect of art, particularly on its critical role; she is fully conscious of her political commitment: "siguiendo un poco la tradición latinoamericana de participación política de los escritores" (A. Dobles 6) [following a bit in the Latin American tradition of political participation of its writers] and cites Darío in her explanation about the role of the artist:

> De cierta manera el poeta es profeta, como dicen, y entonces esa calidad, esa dimensión de la poesía que le atribuye la gente espontáneamente por la historia que tenemos, por Rubén Darío, por lo que sea, de alguna manera también es una responsabilidad de participación para mí, de ser una voz crítica, de no dejar de hacer análisis crítico, de hacer conciencia crítica de la sociedad. (A. Dobles 6)

> [In a certain way the poet is a prophet, as they say, and so that quality, that dimension of poetry that people attribute to spontaneity because of the history we have, because of Rubén Darío, because of whatever, in a way also indicates a responsibility to participate for me, to be a critical voice, never to stop making critical analysis, to make conscious criticism of society.]

Moreover, art as felt experience implies an aesthetic problem concerning the kinds of feelings art projects or provokes in its audience. Belli parodies the problem in a short dialogue between a lightning bolt, a serpent, and Odaer:

La belleza es como cuando yo aparezco en el cielo e ilumino todo lo que toco—dijo el rayo.
—Pero tú das miedo—dijo la serpiente.
—Mira quién habla—respondió el rayo. (21)

["Beauty is like when I appear in the sky and illuminate everything I touch," said the lightening bolt.
"But you're scary," said the serpent.
"Look who's talking," responded the lightning bolt.]

Certainly Darío would be more inclined to agree with the lightning bolt, that beauty illuminates everything it touches, for beauty, Darío thought, need only exist. But Odaer's response to this humorous exchange is deadly serious: "Yo quiero algo que dé felicidad" (21) [I want something that produces happiness]. Odaer's conception of art, and we can logically assume Belli speaks through him, ultimately agrees with the precepts of beauty and idealism that underpin Darío and the Latin American Modernist movement: "Creo en ese poder de la palabra, extraordinario, de la palabra que nos une a todos; ser parte de esa red" (A. Dobles 6) [I believe in that power of the word, which is extraordinary, of the word that unites us all; to be part of that network].

Perhaps, in addition to Odaer's insistence on creating beauty that imparts happiness, we have the clearest distinction in the debate over the differences between children's literature and adult literature. Certainly, if the production of happiness is the sole criteria for art, much of the adult canon would fail to qualify. But the happily-ever-after convention in children's literature is a firm component of reader expectation, and one that Belli adheres to in this story. Art is fragile, as the wind and the volcanoes point out to Odaer; beauty can be damaged and destroyed, but Odaer counters that it always returns; it never gives up. Thus, art for Belli falls within the Mayan tradition of the natural cycles of rebirth and regeneration as well as Darío's ideal of art as the essence of human dreams and imagination.

Even though "a nadie parece importarle que no exista eso que tu quieres diseñar" (14) [no one seems to care that what you want to create doesn't exist], Odaer firmly believes that the world will be a better place because of his creation. Although he has chafed at the limitations imposed on his artistic potential, he has played within the rules; he has not changed them. Still, he has managed to find his own poetic voice. As Belli talks back to her artistic past, chafing at the limitations imposed by her aesthetic heritage and searching, like Odaer, for her own poetic voice, she inevitably returns to the literature that precedes her. After the decades long political struggle in Nicaragua and elsewhere in Latin America, after all the *testimonios* and revolutionary poetry produced in Central America as the result of the low-intensity wars of the 1970s and 1980s, Belli ultimately returns to Darío in this story for children of all ages and concedes that beauty is its own reward.

8
Politically Correct in Costa Rica
Lara Ríos, Leonardo Garnier, and Carlos Rubio

The best-known writers for children today in Costa Rica are Lara Ríos (1934), Leonardo Garnier (1955), and Carlos Rubio (1968). All three authors have received some international editorial promotion: Ríos through her consistent publication with Editorial Norma, which has distribution points in most of the major cities of Latin America, Garnier through his publication with Mexico's Centro de Desarrollo y Información de la Comunicación y la Literatura Infantiles (CIDCLI), and Rubio through his participation in two UNESCO publications as well as his publications with Editorial Norma. While vastly different from each other in terms of themes, structure, style, and approach, all of them are intent on questioning the boundaries that traditionally and artificially have defined and limited the creation and production of children's literature. They parody classic tales, recapture rapidly disappearing oral traditions, insert their views on polemical social problems, and demonstrate an increasing awareness of ecology, diversity, and global pressures.

Lara Ríos: (Mis)Representing the Other

The most prolific children's writer in Costa Rica today is without a doubt Lara Ríos, the pseudonym for Marilyn Echeverría Zürcher de Sauter, who has been writing steadily for the last thirty years. The granddaughter of famous Costa Rican poet and intellectual Aquileo Echeverría, she received the Carmen Lyra Prize in 1975 for her earliest work, *Algodón de azúcar* (1976) [Cotton candy], a collection of humorous poems. Her real success, however, came with the publication of *Pantalones cortos* [Short pants] (1982), a narrative about a hyperactive little boy, Arturo Pol, who tells his own story by writing in his "every other day" diary ("pormediario"). This book about the problems of growing up in Costa Rica became so popular within the country (some 350,000 copies circulate to date) that Ríos wrote two sequels in the same diary format following Arturo as he grows into adolescence: *Verano de colores* (1990) [Summer of colors] and *Pantalones largos* (1993) [Long pants]. In these novels she confronts issues of drugs and violence, sex and unplanned pregnancies as well as a number of other problems that range from Arturo's hyperactivity to Costa Rica's ecological problems. Her novel *El círculo del fuego blanco* (2000), reminiscent of C.S. Lewis's *Cronicles of Narnia*, continues her symbolic representation of the psychological problems of adolescence. By setting up a parallel cosmology to that of Christianity, she describes the descent into alternative regions of hell where the child is at the mercy of a host of demons.

In what she claimed would be her final novel, *La música de Paul* (2001) [Paul's music], winner of the 2002 Premio Nacional Aquileo J. Echeverría and recently translated into French, she explores the psychological problems of depression, loneliness, and death from a child's perspective. She also moves the setting to Costa Rica's Afro Caribbean community on the Atlantic Coast. With the publication of this short narrative she bade farewell to her literary career:

> Ya maté las hadas y los duendes. Antes los personajes me bailaban en el escritorio y no me dejaban dormir; ahora ni se me aparecen. Creo que ya cumplí con mi deber como escritora. (qtd. in Ugalde)

> [I've killed the fairies and the gnomes now. Before, characters danced before me on my desk and wouldn't let me sleep; now they don't even appear. I believe I've fulfilled my duty as a writer.]

Despite her publicized intentions, however, her retirement did not last long. According to Costa Rican children's literary critic Evelyn Ugalde, "Los duendes la visitaron de nuevo y le inspiraron su nuevo libro 'Las aventuras de Dora la lora y Chico Perico'" [The gnomes visited her again and inspired her new book *The Adventures of Dora the Parrot and Chico the Parakeet*]. This title (2004) was followed by a sequel *Nuevas aventuras de Dora la lora y Chico Perico* (2005) [New Adventures of Dora the Parrot and Chico the Parakeet].

Both books are structurally tied together by a colorfully dressed parrot and her handicapped friend, a parakeet (with a broken wing), who help various child characters come to grips with a variety of physical and psychological problems not often represented in children's literature: mental retardation, blindness, Tourette's Syndrome (from which the author herself suffers), cerebral palsy, paralysis, broken bones, and hyperactivity. The sequel includes stories about children who suffer from autism, deafness, AIDS, asthma, trauma, and dyslexia. Clearly, Ríos is pushing back the limits that have heretofore circumscribed children's literature to safe, wholesome topics and happily-ever-after endings. In addition, she opens up areas of Costa Rica that have previously been invisible to the majority population, for example, the indigenous culture and the precariousness of Costa Rica's ecology.

This sensitivity to the region's pre-Columbian roots focusing particularly on ecology and the Amerindians follows a similar trend in Costa Rican adult literature that has been increasingly concerned with the destruction of the natural environment and the presentation of suppressed or alternate versions of history.[1] Thus, Ríos's preoccupations reflect those of the entire country; issues that adults have suppressed or deferred since the conquest and that now have fallen squarely into the laps of the children: "Nosotros los viejos, morimos con este siglo llevándonos todos los buenos propósitos de las cosas que se pudieron hacer y no se hicieron. Pero a ustedes les toca iniciar el siglo XXI y tienen la responsabilidad de salvar el planeta" (*Pantalones largos* 210) [We old folks will die with this century taking with us all the good intentions of things that could have been done and weren't. But you will begin the twenty-first century with the responsibility of saving the planet].

Ríos does tend to moralize if the opportunity presents, as can be appreciated in the previous quotation. In addition, her unquestioning faith in God as the final answer to every problem sometimes seems heavy-handed. Yet her willingness to discuss previously taboo subjects and her understated humor usually offset her tendency to offer clichéd solutions. In addition, her narratives serve to instigate dialogue in the classroom, within the family, and among peers. What is even more impressive is her willingness to ascribe fundamental value to other kinds of knowledge.

Most notable of her literary production, in this regard, is her incursion into the lesser-known Amerindian cultures of Costa Rica with her novel about the Cabécar, *Mo* (1992) (see fig. 8.1), based on substantial research and a personal experience living in the indigenous community. Often included in primary school suggested reading lists in the country, it precipitated her nomination to the honor list of the International Board of Books for Young People. Despite the novel's popularity and

Figure 8.1. Front cover of *Mo* by Lara Ríos, illustrated by Vicky Ramos (2006). Reprinted courtesy of the publisher, Farben Grupo Editorial Norma.

its appropriation by educators to introduce children to the less visible elements of Costa Rican culture, it has, nevertheless, received some criticism for continuing the colonial tradition of rewriting an existing culture from a position of dominance. Specifically, Costa Rican critic Albino Chacón Gutiérrez accuses her of "una falsa representación cultural" [a false cultural representation], or what is termed in English "a cultural impersonation," assuming a theoretical impossibility[2] of representing the Other authentically and disinterestedly:

. . . convoca un imaginario poderoso y muy activo: penetrar en el mundo de las culturas indígenas es entrar en contacto con las fuerzas originales, mágicas, ir al encuentro de los orígenes, encontrar la unidad esencial, desterrar lo que estaba enterrado. En suma, la escritora organiza un decorado—el de un indio imaginario e imaginado según los estereotipos que alrededor de él se han construido—y cree así un escenario en el que el exotismo, la búsqueda de los orígenes misteriosos y profundos y el encuentro con el Otro indígena son convocados para ratificar lo que nosotros somos, o creemos ser, frente a lo que no somos.

[She convokes a powerful and very active imaginary: to penetrate into the world of indigenous cultures is to enter into contact with original and magical forces, to seek beginnings, to find essential unity, to disinter what has been buried. In sum, the writer sets the scene—that of the imaginary and imagined Indian according to the stereotypes that have been constructed around him—and creates a scenario in which exoticism, the search for the mysterious and profound origins and the meeting with the indigenous Other are convoked to ratify what we are, or believe ourselves to be, in the face of what we are not.]

Chacón Gutiérrez, ultimately, questions her intentions, "[la] redención de los pueblos indígenas" [the redemption of the the indigenous peoples] by exposing the fallacy of the underlying argument: "¿No es el mismo argumento que preside y sirve para justificar, en nuestros días, el hecho de que escritores reutilicen materiales pertenecientes a las tradiciones culturales aborígenes, que luego ellos publican bajo la forma de libros de los que además, se derivan derechos de autor?" [Is it not the same argument that governs and serves to justify today the fact that writers reuse materials belonging to aboriginal cultural traditions that they later publish in the form of books, from which, in addition, they derive royalties?]

While in principle postcolonial theory supports this kind of argumentation,[3] taken to its ultimate consequences, such a line of reasoning may be self-defeating. If marginalized groups are fundamentally mute, then the dominant class has only two possibilities: to ignore or suppress their existence by making the other metaphorically invisible or to misrepresent it given that all representation of the other (including that of adults who write from the perspective of children) can never be, by definition, authentic. That is, if the relationship between center and periphery, self and other, dominant and subaltern can only be seen in the light of how hegemony ignores, suppresses, or misrepresents difference, then all hope for social change becomes moot. While it is clear that the language of the colonizer can never adequately represent the colonized since it can only describe otherness in terms of itself, at least an initial recognition of difference, albeit distorted, focuses the reader's attention on what has previously been invisible to the dominant class and serves to initiate a process of increased awareness and tolerance for multiplicity; that is, it becomes a part of what I have termed in this study as border interaction.

Although Spivak claims that the subaltern cannot speak in a way that can significantly change the relations of power, I wonder whether the problem is really that of the subaltern's inability to speak or of hegemony's inability to listen. Marginalized groups have always made multiple attempts to communicate (Mignolo's "fractured enunciations") that often avoid direct confrontation and circumvent language itself. The only possibility for exploring such lines of communication and spaces for dialogue, however, is for the hegemonic center to acknowledge first and foremost that the periphery exists, that is, to insert the periphery into the dominant discourse, even if at this point it means that hegemony is still basically talking to hegemony. By deconstructing the monolithic myth of the metropolis and acknowledging disagreement, ambivalence, and polyphony within hegemony, the importance of inserting previously muted voices into the discussion increases. At least some elements within the dominant power structure may be able/willing to hear.

Rios's novel is such an attempt to insert these silent and often silenced peripheral groups into the dominant discourse. In so doing, she foments a kind of border interaction, that is, a historical moment when one side reaches out to the other in an attempt, not to represent the other but to learn from him or her, to listen to the border knowledge, fractured though it may be, in order to understand it, not only in hegemonic terms but in the terms and parameters specified by the other. This imagining of oneself *in the place of* the other is vital to any process of social critique.

Ríos has made an honest attempt to listen to the Cabécar first and learn from them, and only then to represent them (as sympathetically as an outsider can) to other members of the dominant class. She even uses as much of the Cabécar language as possible without obscuring the text (sometimes inserting explanatory footnotes), to circumvent the inherent ideological assumptions reflected in the dominant language. Inevitably, however, she has availed herself of the magic, myths, and exoticism asso-ciated with the reigning Indianist imaginary: "soy muy creyencera [de fantasmas], seguro por la gota indígena que me corresponde" [I am very much a believer in spirits, surely because of the drop of Indian blood that I share]. Nevertheless, she is also intent on deconstructing powerful ste-reotypes and myths regarding race, gender, the superiority of Western science over local knowledge or "superstition," and the universality of the Eurocentric worldview.

Her novel *Mo* tells the story of a young Cabécar girl (named Mo) who is learning the oral tradition and history of her tribe from her grandfather, the tribe's *sukia* or shaman. Ríos is careful to present the girl's beliefs and traditions and the grandfather's teachings in a positive light. She guards against condescension, though in so doing, she may indeed fall victim to the other extreme, a certain romantic tone. The young man who is inter-ested in Mo is also learning to become a *sukia* from Mo's grandfather. In addition, he wants to study Western medicine at the university. It should be emphasized, however, that he does not wish to replace his indigenous beliefs and local epistemology with Western science but rather to com-plement them, believing that both cultural approaches will ultimately help his community. Ríos's careful balancing between these cultural con-structions of opposing (and traditionally mutually exclusive) worldviews reflects a growing national consciousness that Costa Rica is much more complex than the white Creole national imaginary that Carmen Lyra and others formulated at the beginning of the twentieth century. With the pluralistic tenets of postmodernism increasingly overturning mod-ernist faith in science, progress, and the superiority of the white race, Lara Ríos finds she has an audience that did not exist a century ago, one that is more willing to tolerate ambivalence and ambiguity, multi-plicity and difference. Ríos, consequently, has positioned herself at the vanguard of a transformation in cultural identity formation, a moment in which the white, Europeanized, dominant culture from the central plateau of Costa Rica has finally begun to acknowledge the existence of "others" within their midst.

Leonardo Garnier: Doing Business with Lions and Giants

Leonardo Garnier is better known for his political prominence in the coun-try than for his children's fiction. He is currently the minister of public education within the Arias administration (2004–2008) and has served in previous administrations as minister of planning. Professionally, he trained as an economist with the New School of Social Research. To date he has written a collection of short stories for adults and two books for children: *Mono Congo y León Panzón* (2001), a fable about a monkey who loves to cook and a fat lion; and his second book, *El sastrecillo ¿valiente?* (2004), in which "un niño de hoy en día cuestiona cada uno de los hechos narrados en el cuento clásico '*El sastrecillo valiente*'" (Garnier's Web page) [a boy of today questions each of the events narrated in the classic story of the "The Brave Little Tailor"].

Garnier's first story *Mono Congo y León Panzón* was written for his two daughters "a las dos monas para las que nació este cuento: Isabel y Marie" [to the two monkeys/cute girls for whom this story was born: Isabel and Marie]. This dedication, however, is conveniently ambiguous since in Costa Rica "mono" means *monkey* but in Spain it means *cute*. As it happens, Mono Congo's great-great-grandfather was a French chef who managed to return to Africa: "aprendí de mi abuelo André, que lo aprendió de su abuelo Pierre, que vivió varios años en París con los Rostchild y las Frufrú, hasta que se enroló con Barnum en un circo, y aprovechó una escala en el Congo Francés para escapar y volver a casa" (*Mono Congo* 52) [I learned from my grandfather André, who learned from his grandfather Pierre who lived for several years in Paris with the Rothchilds and the Fancy Folks until he signed up with Barnum's circus and took advantage of a stop in the French Congo to escape and return home]. Technically, therefore, the story takes place in Africa, but with all the references to Costa Rican foods, "los picadillos," "el chayote," "las vainicas," and the linguistic regionalisms such as the *voceo*, the setting looks and feels just like home. Africa and Costa Rica merge (just as the word *mona* merges the countries of Costa Rica and Spain in the dedication) into a fictional geography that is simultaneously everywhere and nowhere, a land where monkeys cook and animals talk.

The story follows a recurrent structural formula in this region's narrative where an initial confrontation between weak and strong is deferred following the astute promise of the weak to do something for the strong; here the monkey promises to provide the lion with a succulent dish of food if the lion promises not to eat him. On his way to the lion's den with each successive dish of food, he is thwarted by a jungle animal (an alligator, an elephant, a tiger), who eats the dish before he can deliver it to the lion. At the end of the story, after three failed attempts to keep his promise to the lion—who is now about to eat the monkey—he suddenly receives an unorthodox proposal from the lion: "vos podrías darte gusto cocinando exquisiteces para los dos; y yo, con mis colmillos y las garras, te protegería de las amenazas" (55) [you could cook exquisite dishes to your heart's content for the both of us and I, with my saber teeth and claws, would protect you from threats].

The situation is not unlike Costa Rica's precarious relationship with the United States—to which it provides coffee, bananas, cheap labor and technical expertise in return for protection. As the monkey realizes, "Por otro lado . . . no tengo mucho por donde escoger" (57) [on the other hand, I don't have much choice]. That is, both the lion as well as the United States have made the traditional Mafioso offer that cannot be refused. Before the lion can change his mind, the monkey seals the deal with the popular expression among Costa Rican children "¡Chóquela, socio!" (57) [shake on it, partner], a gesture that highlights the underlying economic exchange that forms the basis of the "partnership." Garnier, therefore, concludes as ambiguously as he begins: "Juntos se divertían, en fin, estos amigos peculiares, que aprendieron a vivir . . . cual familiares" (60; ellipses Garnier's) [Together they enjoyed themselves, at last, these peculiar friends, who learned to live . . . like family] (see fig. 8.2).

The power relationship suggested here befits Garnier's training in economics within a context of international capitalism. If Costa Rica is to survive the burgeoning global market, it will have to live with the lion, so to speak:

> A decir verdad, bien que le molestaban los abusos de los grandulones de la selva, que en los últimos días le habían robado macarrones, berenjenas, espárragos y filet. Y si bien León Panzón era uno de ellos, hacer equipo con él sí que podría acabar con estos problemas. (56)

> [To tell the truth, the abuses of the big shots in the jungle who had stolen his macaroni, eggplant, asparagus, and steak really bothered him. And even though Fat Lion was one of them, teaming up with him could end those problems.]

In the jungle of the global market, "little monkeys" (or their products) clearly stand to get eaten by the big players representing international economies. If, however, the "monkey" plays to his strengths[4] and negotiates astutely, then, despite his fundamentally weaker position in

Figure 8.2. Front cover of *Mono Congo y León Panzón* by Leonardo Garnier, illustrated by Hugo Díaz (2001). Reprinted courtesy of the publisher, Farben Grupo Editorial Norma.

comparison with larger, stronger actors in the global economic order, he can ally with powerful partners by offering what he does well and cheaply in return for protection and survival.[5] As long as the monkey keeps cooking for the lion, this tensely constructed "family" relationship (indicated by Garnier's ellipses) is viable. For the time being, at least, it defers the imminent threat of being swallowed up by the rampant lion of global domination.

Garnier's second story *El sastrecillo ¿valiente?* published in the Encuento series of Mexico's Centro de Información y Desarrollo de la Comunicación y la Literatura Infantiles (CIDCLI), an organization dedicated to promoting "children's and young people's literature written by prominent Spanish-speaking authors" (CIDCLI Web page), has placed him among an elite group of established writers. To date he is the only Central American writer, other than Salvadoran Claribel Alegría and Nicaraguan Ernesto Cardenal, who has written for this series that includes such outstanding South American and Spanish authors as Octavio Paz, Nicanor Parra, Álvaro Mutis, Camilo José Cela, Mario Benedetti, and Severo Sarduy.

The narrator of this story, an unnamed father ("Pa"), actually tells two stories at once: (1) the classic story by the Grimm brothers of the little tailor who kills seven flies with one blow, and (2) the story of him telling this tale to his son. What results is a humorous deconstruction not only of the classic text, but also of reader expectations as two generations clash in their reactions to the story, the father who grew up with traditional fairy tales and the son who lives in a postmodern world dominated by information technology and television. The story transcends the generation gap, however, to reveal a much more significant disjunction. Ultimately what is at stake is the fundamental question of identity within the Costa Rican national imaginary. That is, the disagreement reflected in the father's and son's comments about the classic text results from their conflicting views about who they are.

The father has been brought up with the official construction of cultural identity that began to form at the beginning of the twentieth century, that is, that Costa Ricans are peaceful, agrarian, egalitarian, and white (cf. Molina Jiménez, *Costariccense*). Tied to this imaginary is the popular belief that despite their simple and unassuming outward appearance, Costa Ricans are extremely astute and able to maneuver and manipulate their environment for their own benefit. The fact that Costa Rica is a poor, small country justifies, in the national imaginary, its doing whatever it takes in its own defense or to fulfill its needs. The story of the little tailor, therefore, who through wit alone ends up as king, is an appropriate selection for this father to demonstrate to his son the traditional celebration of the trickster's ability to fool others who are visibly richer and more powerful than he.

The tailor's astute manipulation of language, when he claims that he "killed seven with one blow," plays on reader expectations that "seven" refers to "seven men" rather than "seven flies." This fundamental linguistic confusion allows the tailor to outwit both giants and a king. The king has made the classic offer of his daughter's hand in marriage to anyone who can rid the kingdom of the pesky giants. The tailor never really lies; he just does not volunteer the entire truth and permits others to form erroneous conclusions based on partial and deliberately ambiguous information. Given the Cold War context of the last century where Costa Rica, like the little tailor, had to find ways to survive in a world dominated by giant superpowers, this tale is particularly relevant. The tailor waits for his opportunity to take control while the giants fight among themselves. He thus thwarts the coloniality of power (the king) to get what he wants: the hand of the princess and the throne—that is, control over his own realm and his own house. These are the trickster stories that Costa Ricans have told their children for almost a century (see discussion of Lyra in ch. 3).

The little boy who listens to his father's story, however, comes not only from another generation, one that watches seventy channels of television, but from another mentality, less interested in manipulating the dominant powers and more interested in participating along with them in the new economic order. This changing mentality involves a radical overhaul of Costa Rica's construction of its cultural identity. Fundamentally, the boy questions the need for the imaginary's celebration of the trickster figure who can fool larger, richer, more powerful opponents. With a global market dominated by technology, Costa Rica, with its traditionally high level of education, finds that its insertion into the new economic order no longer depends on the image of itself as more astute than its opponents but on its ability to capitalize on its technological expertise. Power is no longer located or locatable by geographical regions or nation states but exists within the intangible and ubiquitous flow of information exchange. The challenge of local participation in the global market, therefore, has changed from a model of confrontation to a model of cooperation.

As Garnier's story begins, the little tailor promises to buy jam from a street vendor and has her haul her products up three flights of stairs only to purchase four ounces. The boy's reaction reflects his compassion and his recognition of this fundamental injustice:

¡Pero eso no es nada, eso me lo como en un recreo! ¿Y para eso la hizo subir los tres pisos, y con toda su carga, y abrir todos los frascos? ¡Qué malo! ¿No le iba a comprar toda la mermelada, pa? Él le dijo que subiera porque le iba a comprar mucho, toda su mercancía, así le dijo. ¿Por qué, pa, por qué le mintió? (*El sastecillo* 4)

[But that's nothing; I eat that during one school recess! And for that he made her climb up three stories, with everything she was carrying, and open all the jars? How awful! Wasn't he going to buy all the jam, Pa? He told her to come up because he was going to buy a lot, all of her merchandise, that's what he said. Why, Pa, why did he lie?]

From the very outset of the story, therefore, Garnier sets up an opposition between trickery, a valuable attribute in Costa Rican culture, and lies, ethically reprehensible behavior. After the tailor kills the seven flies, the boy responds with environmental concerns:

La profe de ciencias dice que no hay que matar a ningún animal; bueno, sólo si es para comérselo . . . y entonces, si matamos así a las moscas, de siete en siete, pues también se van a acabar las moscas y . . . (6)

[The science teacher says that we shouldn't kill animals; well, unless it's to eat them . . . so then, if we kill flies like that, seven at a time, then the flies will become extinct and . . .]

Thus, the boy intervenes at crucial points in the story that have traditionally passed without notice, that have been accepted as givens in a larger narrative of confrontation, to interject the concerns of a changing climate of opinion.

Each segment of the classic story is visually set off by indentation and italics so that the reader has a structured image of the conflict: first an element of the story, then the child's reaction to it. After each segment, the boy questions the father about the tailor's motives and the unstated assumptions behind the story: "¿Por qué lo engañó el sastrecillo?" [Why did the little tailor trick him?]. Instead of admiring the tailor's ability to get something he wants through wit alone, the boy deconstructs the concept of astuteness by repeatedly calling it tricks, lies, and falsehoods. The boy's reaction to the situation reflects an entirely different take on cultural identity construction. From his point of view, instead of fooling the giants or the king, the tailor should have recognized his own value as an artisan and employed the wiser business strategy of capturing the potential clothing market that these two represented:

> ¿No ves que él era un sastre, y que los gigantes eran grandototototes? Si se hubiera hecho amigo de ellos entonces seguro que ellos lo habrían contratado para que les hiciera la ropa . . . y el sastrecillo habría tenido montones de trabajo. Además, si se hubiera hecho su amigo, los gigantes hasta le habrían construido una supersastrería gigante como ellos. (12)

> [Don't you see that he was a tailor and that the giants were really, really, really big? If he had made friends with them, then surely they would have contracted him to make their clothes . . . and the little tailor would have had tons of work. Besides, if he had befriended them, the giants might even have built him a super-sized workshop, as big as they are.]

In regard to the tailor's plan to forget sewing and to become, instead, a soldier in the king's army, the boy evinces the same fundamental concerns regarding identity:

> Pero pa, él no es un soldado, nunca ha sido . . . ¡es un sastre! ¿Por qué quiere estar en el ejército si lo que él sabe es hacer ropa? A lo mejor lo contratan para hacerle todos los uniformes a los soldados . . . eso sería casi tan bueno como ser el sastre del giganterío. (15)

> [But Pa, he's not a soldier, he never has been . . . He's a tailor! Why does he want to be in the army if what he knows how to do is to make clothes? Maybe they'll contract him to make all the soldiers' uniforms . . . that would be almost as good as being the tailor for the giants.]

The son clearly intuits how to do business in the new economic order. The key lies in identifying what one does well and constructing a cultural identity that values those abilities. Despite Costa Rica's traditional construction of itself as different (and better) than the rest of the isthmus, it is not a misplaced section of Europe (the Switzerland of the Americas) and never has been, just as the tailor is not a soldier and never has been.

Taking advantage of a lucrative business opportunity may not make the tailor a king, but it will ensure the tailor's survival. The goal, therefore, is not to resist colonialism through open confrontation or covert astuteness, but rather to carve out a sustainable niche for oneself within the global market, keeping in mind environmental concerns and the needs of marginalized groups.

The disagreement between father and son, utimately, resides in the vision of self—what one is versus what one wants to be:

> . . . pero ¿no ves que él no quería ser más un sastrecillo, que él quería ser un guerrero, un héroe?
> —Pero no tenía fuerza, ni sabía pelear, ni . . .
> —Ah . . . pero ya viste que se pudo enfrentar al gran gigante . . .
> —Porque lo engañó. (16)

> [. . . but don't you see that he didn't want to be a tailor anymore, that he wanted to be a warrior, a hero?
> —But he wasn't strong and he didn't know how to fight or . . .
> —Ah . . . but you saw how he was able to confront the great giant . . .
> —Because he tricked him.]

If getting what one wants is the result of trickery rather than honest participation, then, according to the boy, it is wrong. He is just as critical of the king who makes the tailor a promise with no intention of fulfilling it.

The king wants the tailor to use his legendary "seven at a blow" power to rid the kingdom of giants. Paradoxically, the giants, despite their size, actually represent a marginalized and misunderstood group, another victim of colonialism's genocidal campaigns:

> —Y, si no son malos, ¿por qué les tienen miedo?
> —¡Porque son grandotes! . . . Bueno, pues porque son distintos. (18)

> [—And, if they're not bad, why are they afraid of them?
> —Because they're huge! . . . Well, then because they're different.]

The boy actually loses the thread of the story because of his refusal to buy into the tautological argument that underpins the action of the narrative; that is, giants should be eliminated because they are giants.

The confrontation between the king and the giants, therefore, rather than constituting a natural opposition for the boy, can only be explained by the father in terms of colonialism's propensity for eliminating diversity.

[E]l sastrecillo tenía la misión de acabar con los gigantes y, como no tenía fuerza ni habilidad como para pelear con ellos, pues . . . usó el truco de ponerlos a pelear entre sí. Y no te extrañes tanto porque, la verdad . . . la verdad, los humanos hacemos eso a cada rato. (20)

[The little tailor's mission was to kill the giants and, since he didn't have the strength or the ability to fight them, well . . . he used the old trick of getting them to fight among themselves. And don't seem so surprised because, in truth . . . in truth, we humans do that all the time.]

What seems natural and right in the fictional world of fairy tales, that is, the human right to kill giants, is analogous to the way colonial governments have assumed the right of white people to kill natives. Just as humans are better than giants in the morality of fairy tales, whites are superior to "savages" in the morality of the modern/colonial world.

These naturalized assumptions, that is, those tenets of a worldview that go without question, become the focal point of the boy's postcolonial challenge: "¿Mu . . . muertos? ¿Por la broma del sastrecillo? ¿Muertos?" [D . . . dead? Because of the tailor's trick? Dead?]. The boy is horrified at the extermination of a marginalized group, just as the postmodern world reacts with horror at the systematic elimination, atrocities, and genocide committed against the once "gigantic" indigenous civilizations under colonialism and neocolonialism. As the story proceeds, the tailor captures a defenseless unicorn to satisfy the orders of the king. The boy again questions the ethics of the tailor's actions in the context of the unnecessary destruction of the natural environment.

By the end of the story, the father puts the word hero in quotation marks since the term itself has become contentious. Ultimately, therefore, the boy questions the fundamental point of the tale, the tailor's so-called "valentía" [courage], hence the question marks in the title. How can this story end well, the boy wonders, "si el rey y su hija y todo el mundo sabe que él no es un gran guerrero sino un simple sastrecillo" [if the king and his daughter and everybody else know that he's not a great warrior but only a simple little tailor]? The father's response pits belief against knowledge:

No creás. Muchas veces los seres humanos seguimos teniendo miedo aunque sepamos que no hay razón para tenerlo. En eso de los miedos suele tener mucho más efecto lo que creemos que lo que sabemos . . . y así pasó en este cuento. (26)

[Don't you believe it. Often people continue to fear something even when we know there is no reason for it. In regard to fear, what we believe tends to have a greater impact than what we know . . . and that's what happened in this story.]

The boy, however, remains unconvinced. He simply cannot or will not identify with the tailor, the supposed "hero" of this tale.

Costa Rica's national imaginary of the last century, based on the exploitation of the natural environment and the suppression of marginalized groups, is no longer a viable or acceptable form of self-definition. The boy's rejection of the father's tale in the last line of the story, therefore, suggests a more fundamental questioning, not just of the father's views but also of an entire generation's construction of reality: "–¿Por qué te gustaban tanto estos cuentos?" (26) [Why have you liked those stories so much?]. The worldview that has traditionally explained how Costa Rica fits into the international economic order, therefore, finds itself undergoing a radical transformation. With the process yet unfinished and the outcome uncertain, it remains to be seen how Costa Rica can protect all of its citizens as well as its natural environment by doing business with the lions and the giants and the kings of the new global jungle.

Carlos Rubio: Who are we really?

Undoubtedly one of the most popular and imaginative writers for children today in Costa Rica is Carlos Rubio. Quite prolific, given his youth, he has written a collection of poetry: *La vida entre los labios* (1985) [Life between lips], which won the Joven Creación [young creation] award from La Editorial Costa Rica, two novels, *Escuela de hechicería: Matrícula abierta* (1995) [School of witchcraft: Open registration] and *Papá es un campeón* (2006) [Papa is a champion], and four collections of short stories: *Queremos jugar* (1990) [We want to play], *Pedro y su teatrino maravilloso* (1992)[6] [Pedro and his marvelous theater], which won the Carmen Lyra Prize, *El libro de la Navidad* (2001) [the Christmas book],[7] and *La mujer que se sabía todos los cuentos* (2003) [The woman who knew all the stories]. He also has edited the children's magazine *Revista Infantil Tambor* (1989–1992), contributed to various anthologies, authored didactic and pedagogical material, and had some of his work turned into radio programs, stage productions, and puppet shows. He is currently president of the Costa Rican Institute for Children's and Juvenile Literature [Instituto de Literatura Infantil y Juvenil de Costa Rica], founded in 1979 by Lara Ríos, and offers children's literature courses in the teacher education programs at two of Costa Rica's oldest and most prestigious universities: La Universidad Nacional and La Universidad de Costa Rica.

Rubio is best known internationally for *La mujer que se sabía todos los cuentos* published by Editorial Norma. Highly praised by Costa Rican reviewers,[8] the book took him a decade to write. It includes eight stories based on the lives of prominent women from Latin America (two of whom are from Costa Rica) and is unified structurally by its nameless protagonist, a woman who knows everyone else's stories but who does not know her own. Each of the eight historical figures presented (Sor Juana Inés de la Cruz, Manuela Sáenz, Gabriela Mistral, Frida Kahlo, Carmen Lyra, Alfonsina Storni, Eunice Odio, and Violeta Parra) provides the protagonist with a letter of the alphabet that unscrambled will spell her name, AMERICA, a feminine designation for the continent whose story/history, like those of the women who inhabit it, "[no] ha sido escrita y contada por ella misma sino por otros" (Caamaño Morúa) [has not been written or told by herself but by others]. Based on substantial historical research, the book, according to its author, tells the stories of:

> . . . mujeres que han tejido una identidad para América Latina y que transgredieron la cultura patriarcal . . . la mayoría murieron a causa de ello, llámese suicidio, aislamiento o muerte natural, pero de alguna manera el patriarcado les cobró muy caro su ruptura. (Interview with Blanco)

> [. . . women who have woven the identity of Latin America and who transgressed patriarchal culture . . . the majority died because of it,

whether by suicide, isolation, or natural death, but in some way patriarchy charged them a high price for their rupture.]

Ironically, *La mujer que se sabía todos los cuentos*, which promotes the presence of women who were instrumental in the historical and artistic formation and formulation of the continent, is written by a male. Rubio's sensitivity, however, to the issues of patriarchy have shielded him so far from accusations that he may have misrepresented, appropriated, or impersonated these women's stories:

Siento que es un libro escrito por la mano de un varón pero desde la perspectiva de las mujeres. Fue un trabajo casi actoral, porque los actores se despersonalizan y prestan su cuerpo a un personaje que los habita temporalmente. (Interview with Muñoz)

[I feel that it is a book written by the hand of a man from the perspective of women. It was almost a work of acting, in the sense that actors depersonalize themselves and let their bodies be inhabited temporarily by another character.]

In fact, one Costa Rican critic even goes so far as to submit that the female characters in this book speak "con voz propia" (Méndez Garita, "Ese hilo") [with their own voice], a paradox indeed. In another interview, however, Rubio reverses his metaphor about the writing hand:

En este libro se aplican las teorías de género sobre cual es la mano que escribe, independientemente de la sexualidad, porque es la escritura lo que cuenta, y me atrevo a asegurar que la que escribe es la mano femenina. (Interview with Blanco)

[In this book we must apply the theories of gender about the hand that writes independently of its sexuality, because it is the writing that counts, and I dare say that the writing hand is feminine.]

Clearly, Rubio is aware of the theoretical concerns involved when a man tells a woman's story.

One of the premises of this book, however, is that all representation is to a certain extent misrepresentation. Distortion is an inevitable consequence of the process of describing the other given that all representation is an imputation of meaning to an alleged external reality from the perspective of the self who describes it. Certainly, no one can any longer innocently claim that his or her representations of external "realities" are objective, true, or disinterested. A woman's pain, resentment, or knowledge of her marginalized status, just as a man's guilt, complacency, or cynicism are intervening variables in the perceptions of the same social conditions that mediate their descriptions. In fact, a man and a woman who share similar conventions are more likely to represent an object of analysis in a similar fashion, than two women who hold disparate assumptions about the same world they are representing in their writings. As Domitila so bluntly challenged over thirty years ago, "¿de qué igualdad vamos a hablar entre nosotros? Si usted y yo no nos parecemos, si usted y yo somos tan diferentes. Nosotros no podemos, en este momento, ser iguales, aún como mujeres . . ." (qtd. in Franco, "Si me permiten hablar" 109) [what equality are we going to talk about among ourselves. When you and I are not anything alike, when you and I are so different. We cannot, at this time, be equal, not even as women . . .]. Furthermore, representation is mediated by language, culture, worldview, historical moment, and perhaps most significantly, the power differential.

My argument throughout, however, has been to demonstrate the periodic attempts of individuals to defy such limitations through significant border interactions. Rubio's effort to bring forward women's views of their realities and concerns, therefore, should not be seen as another male invasion or appropriation of what is fundamentally female, but rather as an insertion of women's stories into a predominately male-centered history of the continent. In this case a male author has made an honest attempt to understand and listen to women before inscribing their histories into stories for children. That is, Rubio makes a concerted effort to liberate himself from the critical position that argues for an "essential" difference between men and women.

Rubio also questions the label that would limit his writing to a juvenile audience. On more than one occasion, he has challenged the convention, reinforced by academics and the market, of categorizing literature according to the age of the audience: "Lo que hago es escribir para mí mismo, escribo el libro que me gustaría leer y cuando está listo el editor decide a qué público va dirigido" (interview with Muñoz) [What I do is write for myself; I write the book I would like to read and when it's ready, the editor decides what audience it fits]. Like Martí, Rubio emphasizes the need to use language "en donde ninguno de los dos se subestima o se considera inferior al otro, en donde se da una relación horizontal. El reto no es qué se dice, sino cómo se dice" [in which neither of the two under-value the other or is considered inferior to the other, in which there is a horizontal relationship. The challenge is not in what is said, but in how it is said]. In other words, he posits his writing as a dialogue, and like Martí who urged his younger readers to correspond with him through his magazine, Rubio invites and posts responses from his readers via his personal Web page.[9]

It is not only that Rubio tackles difficult topics (divorce, suicide, rampant consumerism, neocolonialism, police brutality, even memories of the holocaust of Hiroshima), but that he is able to speak on various levels, not just to children but also to adults. His vision as well as his language is plural, allowing his readers to enter various planes of reality simultaneously. For example his first novel, *Escuela de hechicería: Matrícula abierta*,[10] blends into one multivoiced, interactive whole: neighborhood children, an old woman who has been marginalized as a "bruja" [witch], spirits of the indigenous past, magically real animals with psychological phobias, and foreigners who plan to take economic control over the country. Ultimately, Rubio's story is a retelling of the conquest narrative but with a different outcome, one in which the children protagonists together with the natural and spiritual worlds are able to defeat the intrusive would-be neocolonial power. The magically real character of the story, rather than limiting Rubio's audience to children, actually expands it to readers of all ages.

In Rubio's version, the intruder, Doctor Silentio, represents the dangers of a stealthily encroaching global economy, rapidly turning everyone into robot-like consumers. His name reflects the sophistication of his training as a "doctor" in the discipline of control, that is, technology, and "silent" because of technology's "invisibility." Since it is impossible to locate this emerging power geographically, it is also impossible to talk to it. Significantly, the super mall that Doctor Silentio is building to sell his Coca-Cola-like product, Total Silentio, is shaped like a castle. Dr. Silentio, the would-be king, as did other colonial powers before him, intends to silence the populace, as the name of his product allegorically indicates, by denying and eliminating difference:

Los empleados adoptaron un aire marcial. Parecía que ninguno era más alto ni más bajo. Ni más gordo ni más delgado. Todos caminaban

igual y miraban igual. Sus movimientos eran coordinados y no nece-
sitaban dialogar entre sí. Esos eran los efectos del Total Silentio.
(*Escuela de hechicería* 115)

[The employees adopted a martial air. It appeared that no one was
taller or shorter, fatter or thinner. All of them walked in the same
way and looked the same. Their movements were coordinated and
they didn't need to talk amongst themselves. Those were the effects
of Total Silentio.]

The children protagonists immediately realize the extent of the problem.
As the community degenerates into technologically controlled androids,
they lose their sense of humanity. That is, they forget who they are: "Lo
más importante ahora es librar a nuestro pueblo de la desmemoria" (54)
[The most important thing now is to free our community from its amne-
sia (literally "dismemory"—the negative of memory)].

Cultural cohesiveness in Central America and the Caribbean, as we
have seen in previous chapters, is tied in part to memory, tradition, and
the struggle to recover and identify with the indigenous past. Costa Rica,
compared to the rest of the region, has had a particularly difficult time
resurrecting these indigenous roots since the national imaginary formed
at the beginning of the twentieth century emphasized the racial whiteness
of Costa Rica, its European ancestry, and its uniqueness (racially) on the
isthmus. The counterpart to this "blanqueamiento" [whitening], as Costa
Rican historian Ivan Molina Jiménez calls it, has been to insist upon
the comparative nonexistence of indigenous groups in Costa Rica during the colony and the self-imposed isolation of the few scattered extant
Amerindian populations in the wilderness of the mountainous rain forest. For years Costa Rican children were brought up with the impression
that the Indians were unwilling to collaborate in the national project.

Nevertheless, with the increasing intellectual awareness that certain voices in Costa Rica's history have been systematically muted
(women, Afro Caribbeans, Amerindians), contemporary Costa Ricans
have, for the most part, been making a concerted attempt to rein-
sert these peripheral groups into the national discourse in a process
of (re)self-identification and self-definition that aims to include previously marginalized members of society into the popular imaginary.
This reformulation of Costa Rican cultural identity, a century after its
initial invention, aims not only to recognize but also to celebrate the

complexity and the plurality of Costa Rican culture and to look for commonalities rather than differences with the rest of the region.

Rubio goes one step further, however. In addition to the historically suppressed voices of women, blacks, and Indians, Rubio adds the voices of children themselves, children who will become adults in a marginalized region of the world. The story that gives its title to his collection, *Queremos Jugar*,[11] is a vocal protest by children to defend their right to play, that is, to protect their right to be children. In this story, just as in *La mujer que se sabía todos los cuentos*, the children speak metaphorically "in their own voice." They make signs and placards and they march in public protest against the expropriation of their neighborhood playground, which has been fenced off for construction. Furthermore, the new owners of the land are foreigners and whiter even than Costa Rica's traditional perception of itself: "Nunca habían visto a nadie con la piel tan blanca y los ojos tan azules" (50) [They had never seen anybody before with such white skin and such blue eyes]. Clearly, Rubio, in response to the systematic whitening of Costa Rica's national imaginary during the previous century, is intent on darkening Costa Rica's perception of itself, uniting instead with the rest of the Central American region in contrast to the perceived "whiteness" of Europe and the United States.

The government claims that foreign investment is good for the economic development of the country, echoing the arguments supporting the controversial TLC (Tratado de Libre Comercio)—CAFTA (Central American Free Trade Act) with the United States:

> . . . su presencia significaba un gran avance para la comunidad y que para ellos [los niños/as], dejar de divertirse allí sólo representaba un pequeño sacrificio por el bien de su gente. (52)

> [. . . their presence signified great progress for the community, and for them (the children) to give up playing there only meant making a little sacrifice for the good of the people.]

The children have to content themselves with a small lot that the community, with the help of the foreign investors, turn into a new playground. The exchange, however, is uneven and reminiscent of the minor concessions empires make to protesting colonies. Nevertheless, when the construction is finished and the wall around the old lot comes down, the children realize that the foreigners have built a military base, a metaphorical power base within the country: "vieron a centenares de hombres uniformados que sostenían metralletas. Y salieron tanques. Y aviones que disparaban proyectiles explosivos" (56) [they saw hundreds of men in uniforms holding machine guns. And tanks rolled out. And airplanes shot explosive projectiles.]. In a caustic understatement, Rubio concludes: "Los niños comprendieron que los soldados no venían solamente a construir puentes y hospitales" (56) [The children understood that the soldiers had not come only to build bridges and hospitals].

Rubio is writing at a historical moment in which the economic order is changing qualitatively from a scenario of rich nations (controlling) and poor nations (controlled) to a more illusive, intangible, nongeographic, and non-national technological managing of global economies and market participation. That is, the controlling structures that interact with controlled resources are defined not by statehood but by their function in the new economic order. Those functions are no longer located within discreet geographic boundaries but in the alienating flow of billions of packets of information that threaten to turn people into objects of cybernetic management. The resulting power relationship forms a new kind of "invisible" cybernetic colonialism, hard to identify and harder still to resist. In this story, therefore, the soldiers do not invade from the outside as they would in a traditional neocolonial takeover but erupt from within. The children who confront the soldiers at the end of Rubio's story with their demand that "queremos jugar" [we want to play], consequently, project a vision of themselves into the future as adults who will, in their turn, demand to play in the game of globalization, technology, and world markets and who will resist being dispossessed of their natural resources, their "playgrounds" by more powerful players.

Rubio's most recent book, *Papá es un campeón*, takes an apparent hiatus from sociopolitical problems to concentrate instead on individual/family issues, specifically the difficult relationship between a boy, Isaac, and his overly dominant father, Abraham. The biblical names, of course, are not incidental. Interestingly, the book is dedicated to Rubio's own father: "A mi padre, Carlos Alberto Rubio Vargas, quien aún anota goles en alguna cancha del universo" [To my father, Carlos Alberto Rubio Vargas, who still makes goals on some soccer field in the universe]. The father in this story is a rabid soccer fan, as Costa Ricans still tend to be; the novel is structured like a soccer game, divided into two halves ("tiempos"), and the title itself shows the boy's admiration for his father in terms of a soccer competition. The story is narrated in third person from Isaac's perspective, and his problems with his father are immediately apparent. The father likes soccer; Isaac likes the arts. The father is athletic; the boy wears glasses and is clumsy. Recently divorced from Isaac's mother, Abraham only sees the child on Saturdays and forces him to go to soccer practice where he is constantly disappointed by Isaac's performance.

The relationship between father and son in this novel mimics in the extreme the colonial relationship inherent in the socialization of children. Isaac's father wants a son in his own image; he belittles the boy's interests and growing identification with the poet who lives across the street; he tries to change what he does not like about the boy (civilize him), and devalues Isaac's unusual artistic abilities. The two simply do not see the world in the same way. Then the father becomes terminally ill, and everything changes. Colonial forces are dying, ceding to a new globalism where what counts is not Costa Rica's previous ability to "play in the World Cup" but its ability to make itself heard through its cultural contributions. The country's recent emphasis on "ecotourism" and its promotion of autochthonous culture, for example, underline this fundamental change and revaluation of its human and natural resources.

As Isaac's father grows steadily weaker and more dependent on his son for company and support in the second half of this soccer game, he slowly learns to value the boy and vice versa. Isaac also grows closer to his father during this time of caretaking. Similarly, contemporary Costa Ricans find themselves in a period of transition and transformation in terms of understanding who they are. The initial conflict between opposing views of the self, the old and the new, the traditional and the avant-garde, has been substituted by a rapprochement of the two as the new cultural imaginary tries to understand and integrate the old.

Intertwined with the story line is what at first appears to be a magically real context, a narrative approach that has almost come to be expected of contemporary Latin American literature. Rubio, however, puts his own spin on the phantasms that appear to Isaac. They are not "really" magical, although they are invisible to others. Nor is Isaac schizophrenic, seeing things that are not there. Once he meets and befriends his neighbor, the poet, and discovers that he also can see Isaac's apparitions, we adult readers begin to understand what the child readers have undoubtedly intuited all along. The apparitions that Isaac sees are real; they belong, however, to

— ¿Se te
ocurre pen-
sar cómo será
la vida dentro de
trescientos años? —pregunta Pedro—. Es muy posible
que ya   no existan cocinas porque habrán máquinas que
prepa-   rarán los alimentos sin intervención de los seres
huma-   nos. A lo mejor no habrán automóviles, sino peque-
ños objetos volantes que trasladarán a la gente de un
lado a otro. Es   muy po-   sible
que tampoco e-   xistan   libros
y eso sería   muy
aburrido.

Figure 8.3. Text shaped like a key from *Pedro y su teatrino maravilloso*, by Carlos Rubio (1990). Reprinted courtesy of the publisher, Editorial Costa Rica.

a non-ordinary reality, a parallel but other reality. That is, Isaac, like artists in general, Rubio implies, sees the world in a different way.

This ability to see what is invisible to everyone else places a responsibility on the artist to include this "other reality" in his or her artistic construction of the world. It also permits Isaac a unique experience when his father dies. He sees his father's spirit leave its body, grab a soccer ball and soccer shoes, and take off for the "País del Sueño" [the land of dreams]: "sin desprenderse del balón, levantaba la mano y se despedía del niño" (200) [without letting go of the ball, he raised his hand in farewell to the boy]. Isaac, clearly Rubio's own alter ego, likewise bids farewell to his father: "Adiós, papá campeón, mi capitan" (201) [Good-bye, Papa the Champion, my captain]. In this psychological catharsis, Isaac is able to forgive his father for his previous treatment of him and for his errors of vision in the past, just as Costa Ricans in general, must confront their heritage—that is, look backwards—in order to move on.

Rubio's playful sense of humor, the musicality of his language, and his old-fashioned ability to tell a good story are attributes enough to merit following the career of this promising young writer. Yet his real contribution is his ability to show his readers other perspectives, other ways of seeing and knowing. His experiments with the formal presentation of his narratives range from introducing alternative endings to manipulating the typesetting to form visual images. The introduction to one of his stories is formatted into the image of a key (see fig. 8.3). Another story begins with the image of an umbrella created from text (see fig. 8.4)

A
las nubes
se les ha ocurrido
reventarse en esta tarde.
Los niños no podrán ir a la plaza
a escuchar los cuentos de Pedro.   Sólo
Eugenia, una chica de doce años, ha llegado,
con su pequeño títere y su diario. ¿Querés
co-
no-
cer
lo
que
le
ha
con   ta
do?

Figure 8.4. Text shaped like an umbrella from *Pedro y su teatrino maravilloso*, by Carlos Rubio (1990). Reprinted courtesy of the publisher, Editorial Costa Rica.

Like Darío and the modernist poets of the nineteenth century, the emphasis in Rubio's aesthetics is clearly on the visual image, but whereas Darío believed that art should recreate the beautiful, celebrate the ideal, and value the sublime, Rubio's aesthetics are clearly linked to a postmodern ethic. Art for Rubio recreates the Other, celebrates difference, and values alternative ways of perceiving those realities that we imagine and construct to give our lives meaning. Ultimately, Rubio is dealing with the agony of a dying national imaginary and the birth of a new space for Costa Ricans to define who they are.

All three writers, Ríos, Garnier, and Rubio, therefore, form part of a new generation of Costa Rican writers who recognize the need for a revision and a reformulation of the naturalized assumptions that have traditionally limited discussions surrounding questions of national identity, values, culture, purpose, and policy. Their writing strives to be inclusive and politically correct, neither minimizing nor ignoring difference, but rather incorporating it into the national discourse. Thus, their work implies a change in the fundamental challenges now facing countries with a colonial history. It is no longer sufficient to fool the more powerful figures who control the sociopolitical and economic order so that the underdog can experience the fleeting pleasure of one-upmanship, beating the master at his own game. Rather the challenge is to play a new game, to construct a national imaginary that reconfigures individual, national, and cultural identity in terms of a revised concept of unity based not on an artificial homogeneity, but on the potential strengths to be rediscovered and revalued in plurality and diversity.

9
Conclusion
Juan Bobo's True IQ

> . . . jamás volvieron a preguntarse si Juan Bobo era tan bobo como
> parecía[. . . they never again asked themselves if Juan Bobo was as
> foolish as he seemed]. (Rosario Ferré, *Sonatinas*)

Central America recently celebrated the twentieth anniversary of the sign-
ing of the Esquipulas II Peace Accords, for which Costa Rican president
Oscar Arias won the Nobel Peace Prize in 1987. A strange historical junc-
ture finds both Oscar Arias and Daniel Ortega once again presidents of
their respective countries, Costa Rica and Nicaragua. Both originally left
office in 1990 ushering out an era of U.S. military presence and economic
control in the region. Both had presided during the worst economic cri-
sis since 1939. The International Monetary Fund ruled the day, requir-
ing compliance with U.S. economic objectives in response to Central
America's gigantic foreign debt. But as the decade came to a close, the
Sandinistas were voted out of office in Nicaragua, signifying a turn away
from leftist politics and ending U.S. support for the counterrevolutionary
movement. Today, with both Arias and Ortega once again at the helms of
their countries after a hiatus of over fifteen years, it is as though history
were somehow repeating itself, except that the actors are older and quite
a bit grayer.

Coincidentally, or perhaps not, this political twosome, despite their
opposing views then and now, have been at the public forefront at two
of the most critical moments in Central American history, as one era
ends and another begins. As the imperial might and economic influence of the United States dwindles in the region, it is replaced by a new
sphere of influence, no longer controlled by the superpowers or trans-
national monopolies. Instead, a rapidly developing cybernetic technology is changing how the world does business and how people relate to
one another. Then, as now, Arias and Ortega reflect the region's opposing
approaches to these changes: Costa Rica once again looking for consensus, for how to place itself strategically to play the new global game, and
Nicaragua, more contentious, allying itself with Venezuela's Hugo Chávez
and the new political left, reluctant to play at all. Their differences notwithstanding, both men find they are leading countries in the process of

fundamental transformation, undergoing not just economic adjustments to a new world order, but essential revisions in who they are.

The formation of national identity, crucial to the consolidation of Latin America's new nation states during the last century, was an ongoing and complex process of exclusion and inclusion that responded both to official designs within each country and popular perceptions. Children's literature in Central America and the Caribbean, therefore, initially played a fundamental role in socializing children to function within an international framework made up of superpowers and smaller nations. While the official literature tried to integrate children into the dominant system and to teach them to be good colonial subjects, the traditional oral folklore managed to escape colonial control and propagated the unofficial lessons children heard for over a century insinuating how to deal with the existing colonial or neocolonial power structure.

The trickster character, a stock character in many national literatures from around the world, took a particularly virulent form in the Caribbean that spilled over into Central America in the guise of the Juan Bobo stories, folktales constructed "using a mixture of Christian religion; African, Spanish, and Indian traditions; folkloric politics; and popular beliefs" (Lastra 9). That is, these stories are an eclectic mixture grounded in the three racial groups that formed the region. Juan Bobo, the apparent town fool, is a man of humble origins who manages to circumvent traditional barriers, manipulate the system, and deconstruct the dominant language itself to expose the hypocrisy and find the inherent weaknesses in the colonial/imperial power structure, permitting him to get the better of stronger opponents. This character, usually described as uncultured, not handsome, with a dominant mother, reflects a rather thinly disguised colonial model: the dominance of the mother country (Spain) in relation to her rather ugly offspring (Latin America). The character's name varies throughout the region and has provoked some analysis by anthropologists and folklorists: his first name Juan [John] has roots, of course, in the Christian tradition and may suggest some intertextual allusions to the great Johns of Spanish literature (Juan Ruiz de Alarcón, Don Juan Tenorio, Juan sin Miedo) (see Lastra 9). His last name, Bobo, with variations throughout Latin America (Simple, Animala) just means "stupid." Essentially, however, he functions as a Latin American Everyman. As such, despite his apparent foolishness, his underlying ability to trick or revenge himself on more powerful opponents (invariably symbols of authority—his own mother, the judge, the king) positions him in the center of a process of cultural identity formation, particular to Puerto Rico, but easily generalized to the region based on a common colonial and neocolonial experience.

The link between Juan Bobo and Puerto Rican cultural identity has been noted by numerous Puerto Rican anthropologists (see Lastra). Manrique Cabrera, for example, describes Juan Bobo as a character who mirrors traits in the population of the countryside:

> The character of Juan Bobo, under all its forms and costumes, seems to show, prima facie, an evolution in the stories where he is the main character. The simple fool transforms himself into a person that pretends to be a numskull, using his foolishness as a disguise. This evolutionary slanting seems to reflect the assimilation of a trait attributed to the jíbaro's psychic [sic]. It refers to what has been called "jaibería," an attitude which feigns dullness to throw off those who come near. It is a defensive weapon whose ultimate efficacy is worth investigating (Manrique Cabrera, qtd. in Lastra 13).

My argument here, however, is twofold: one, that Juan Bobo, as Everyman, represents a broader range of Puerto Rican culture than just the *jíbaro* or the country farmer, and two, that he not only reflects traits already present in the culture, but also directly contributes to the formation and propagation of those traits, especially as the oral stories about him have been transferred to print versions aimed at children. Although Lastra claims that "for didactic reasons, the Juan Bobo character that mainly appears in children's literature is the fool whose cardinal flaw is stupidity, while the rogue who satirizes society, swindles others, or has amorous adventures lives primarily in oral traditions or scholarly publications" (14), I have not found that to be the case,[1] particularly in Rosario Ferré's collection for children, where the roguish elements of Juan Bobo's character certainly come to the fore.

Furthermore, although the internal power structure in Puerto Rico relegates the *jíbaro* to the bottom of the social ladder, making him the most visible representation of exclusion and marginalization, it is also true that the Island as a whole suffers from a similar marginalization on a larger scale, which, without diminishing the complexity of the internal power structure, encourages cultural cohesion through opposition. By extension, the recognition by the rest of the region of the commonalities in the area's colonial experience and marginalized status underlies a regional cohesion or imaginary that supersedes national barriers and has made Juan Bobo, for one, a well-known figure outside the confines of Puerto Rico. This marginalized Other par excellence uses his intellectual dullness as Manrique Cabrera claims as "a defensive weapon" to thwart the aims and ambitions of colonialism. Whether in practice this technique is effective or not is of less importance, it seems to me, than its role in offering the population a cultural imaginary capable of preserving not only regional identity but also individual self-esteem.

Several versions of one tale underline this argument. Ferré tells the story of Juan Bobo who, before a judge, accuses some flies of not paying him for stealing his molasses (in other versions, his meat). The judge gives him permission to whack the next fly he sees. Thus, when a fly lands on the judge's nose, Juan Bobo whacks him. One popular version sends Bobo to jail as a result; another rewards him by having the judge pay the fly's "debt" to avoid being hit again. In Ferré's version the judge just pretends to ignore Juan Bobo's muttered complaints: "¡Justicia, ni qué justicia! ¡Si ya se sabe que pal pobre no hay justicia!" (*Sonatinas* 54) [Justice, what justice! Everybody knows that for the poor there's no justice!]. The ultimate consequence for Juan Bobo in this story, however, is less important than the satisfaction the listener/reader experiences when Juan hits the judge. The fact that all of the versions agree on this central point emphasizes the underlying message that authority can be successfully affronted (although perhaps not directly confronted) and justifies the revenge taken. As Guerra argues "Behind the facade of this 'jíbaro manso' lurks the mind of a Puerto Rican superhero whose wit, brilliance, thespian proclivities, and bravery in the face of danger make him the ideal seeker and defender of justice for those who experience little of it in their real lives" (Guerra, qtd. in Lastra 13). The same, of course, might be said of the rest of Latin America.

In a further analysis of his name, Lastra posits that Bobo is stuck within his marginalized status, no matter what he does (just as Latin America is):

He will, by implication of his name, never move out of the classification of being an "outsider," being "lower" than others. For example, the stories begin by placing him in a category of fools, and (almost all) end with Juan Bobo still being called a fool, even though in some folktales he marries the king's daughter or acquires some fortune. So Juan Bobo's name seems to suggest that some things never change. (17)

Clearly, Latin America has no possibility of ever acquiring the "culture" of Europe and will always be considered an outsider and "lower than others" (read Europeans) within a Western definition of what constitutes "culture" and legitimate knowledge. Leaders from the third world routinely appear as uncultured buffoons and fools in European presses. Juan Bobo inevitably acts the part of the uncultured simpleton, an easy target for exploitation, but just as inevitably enacts his revenge. His apparent weakness, therefore, when read in reverse becomes his strength.

Juan Bobo's proclivity to interpret what is said to him literally (and to make social errors as a result) highlights the notion that what colonial powers say is not necessarily what they mean: "¡Ay Mai, no me pegue, no me pegue! ¡Si yo no hice más que lo que usté me dijo!" (Ferré, *Sonatinas* 64) [Oh, Ma, don't hit me, don't hit me! I just did what you told me to!]. His understanding of the literal level of the dominant language not only deconstructs the language of power but also highlights the hypocrisy within colonial institutions. In one story, for example, Ferré takes aim at the Church. Juan Bobo's mother gives him instructions about how to recognize the cathdral since Juan wants to go to Mass and she cannot go with him. He takes her description literally (a place where lots of people go in and out) and ends up instead at a party celebrating a baptism where he eats and drinks and enjoys himself. When he actually does end up at the church for Mass the next time he goes, he is sure he has gone to the wrong place since all they offer him to eat is "una galleta bien jincha" (57) [a really large cracker] and when he asks for more, he is beaten. The Church clearly does not "fill" Juan Bobo, whereas in the party for the baptism, he is included, fed, and made to feel welcome even though he knows no one in the house.

In another story where Juan Bobo is invited to a banquet "en casa de una gente muy fina" (Ferré 58) [in the house of some rich people], his mother gives him specific instructions on how to behave; one of her warnings is to eat very little. In Bobo's frustration at not being allowed to eat his fill, he exposes the absurdity of "civilized" behavior and declares his independence "¡Banquete ni qué banquete! ¡Si en casa e la gente rica el pobre tie' que aprendel a sel tan fino que come sin habel comío, y encima lo obligan a decil no quiero más, yo me voy pa' mi casa y que no me vuelvan a invital!" (60) [Banquet! What banquet! In rich people's houses, the poor have to learn to be so cultured that they eat without having eaten and, to top matters off, they have to say that they don't want any more. I'm going home, and I hope never to be invited again!].

In other words, if starvation is what having culture really means, then Juan Bobo and the marginalized Other he represents would prefer to have none of it.

Thus, Juan Bobo exposes the hypocrisy of the centers of colonial authority: the Church, the judicial system, and the upper class. In addition, Ferré writes what Bobo says phonetically, specifically, substituting "l" for "r" and dropping word endings or "d" between vowels (e.g., *tie'* for *tiene* and *comío* for *comido*). The use of such regionalized Spanish literally deconstructs the so-called "mother" tongue and turns it into a weapon against itself.

These qualities of Juan Bobo, the paradoxically astute fool, split into two separate characters in the Central American folktales of Tío Coyote and Tío Conejo, folktales that have been recorded from Southern Mexico to Costa Rica. In fact, the figure of the coyote has been rigorously studied, beginning with anthropologist Claude Lévi-Strauss.

> A partir de la hispanización, [el coyote] fue transformando sus significaciones en el imaginario colectivo, de deidad creadora a demonio destructor; y el mestizaje le fue dando nuevos matices; el demonio destructor devino en el conquistador y, por extensión, en todos los poderosos. (Rodríguez Valle 110)

> [As a result of Hispanization, (the coyote) began changing its meanings in the collective imaginary, from a creative deity to a destructive devil; and *mestizaje* gave it new nuances; the destructive demon evolved into the conquistador and, by extension, into anyone powerful.]

The coyote, despite his destructive potential, has all of Juan Bobo's simplicity and gullibility without his hidden astuteness. This last aspect of Bobo's character is reflected in the coyote's counterpart Uncle Rabbit, physically much weaker than the coyote, but ultimately more powerful.

> Tío Conejo representa, dentro del mundo de las clases dominadas, un personaje clásico impugnador de valores, al que se han transferido una serie de acciones, en especial la de vencer al poderoso haciendo uso del hechizo de la astucia y la jactancia. El conejo es sinónimo de grandes hazañas; las clases subalternas se ven reflejadas en sus acciones. (Rodríguez Valle 96)

[Uncle Rabbit represents, within the world of the suppressed classes, a classic character, a fighter for values, to whom a series of actions have been attributed, especially that of triumphing over the powerful by tricking them with astuteness and boastfulness. The rabbit is the synonym of great feats; the subaltern classes are reflected in his actions.]

The fundamental situation of Uncle Rabbit and Juan Bobo is too similar to be overlooked: the weak figure getting the better of, or at least exacting his revenge upon, the strong one, providing the listener/reader with a good laugh at the expense of the dominant group. As Bertrand Barbe notes regarding the Nicaraguan versions: ". . . cómica e infantil para nuestra mentalidad contemporánea, [el folklore nicaragüense] sirve en realidad por medio de la broma popular, a difundir ampliamente las creencias en la mentalidad colectiva" (4) [while comic and infantile for our contemporary mentality, Nicaraguan folklore really functions by using this popular joke to disseminate broadly the beliefs of the collective mentality]. This pattern repeats itself in other third world literatures, as well. For example, the greedy West African trickster spider Anancy crops up in Belize's children's literature only to be outwitted by Brother Rabbit (*Rabbit Play Trik Pahn Hanaasi*). As Rodríguez Valle explains, "La astucia no solamente sirve para eludir al coyote sino para vencerlo y torturarlo; se vuelve un juego entre el listo y el tonto, en el cual, además de la elaboración que significa poder vengarse del poderoso, se expresa una enseñanza de supervivencia" (98) [Astuteness not only serves to elude the coyote but also to triumph over him and to torture him; it becomes a game between the smart and the dumb, in which in addition to the elaboration that signifies the ability to revenge oneself on the powerful, resides a lesson in survival].

This scenario that repeats in the oral tradition throughout the area, examples of which we have seen in Carmen Lyra's Costa Rican versions, revalues local knowledge and facilitates and encourages the psychological survival of an entire marginalized population—some members of which are more marginalized than others without doubt—by boosting the self-esteem of a group that has existed on the periphery for more than four centuries. Neither fully European nor fully Indian, Martí's "hombres naturales" have had to create defense mechanisms to protect their integrity and selfhood. Folktales passed from adults to children, consequently, form the backbone of this defensive system. As Lastra reminds us, "Even if traditional markers that have served in the past to establish cultural boundaries are deconstructed, old and new stories coexist and are transmitted through a folkloric network, serving as shifting boundaries that outline a cultural identity. . . . [I]n any language our stories define who we are" (20).

The common theme in the children's stories and folktales from the last century, therefore, is that astuteness, within a colonial framework, is a more valuable attribute than brute power. As the century comes to a close, however, this theme is undergoing revision just as the very relations of power based on the colonial/imperial experience are shifting. The effect of local information and knowledge that can be spread instantaneously throughout the world, with all of the advantages and disadvantages that such advancing technology implies, changes the fundamental relations and structures of power that have been in place for centuries. With this destabilization of the location of knowledge, the superpowers are losing their privileged status and epistemological control to a broader, more inclusive power base. As a result, an implicit consensus among contemporary children's writers is emerging that challenges the validity and the usefulness of the trickster theme. The ability to outwit more powerful opponents, while always an attractive idea, especially to children who yearn (like Juan Bobo or Tío Conejo) to fool adults, seems less important today than the ability to be a player in global "games" at all levels. Thus, there is a move toward inclusion rather than exclusion in our social relations, a shift that is reflected in contemporary attitudes of "political correctness," multiculturalism, and concern for the environment, themes that are increasingly mirrored in the works of contemporary children's writers in the area.

The Dominican story of the Ciguapa, for example, referred to in the introduction of this study, undergoes a radical change in a recent version (2000) by Leibi Ng, in which a little girl dreams about being a Ciguapa. As it turns out, we learn that her mother actually was a Ciguapa who died shortly after the birth of her daughter. Before she dies, however, she is relieved to see that her daughter's feet do not point backwards, "sonriendo al comprobar que su niñita había nacido con los pies derechos, como su padre" [smiling when she made sure that her little daughter had been born with her feet pointing forward, like her father's]; she will not suffer as the mother has for her difference. The message is ambivalent: the mother wants the little girl to look like everyone else, but the little girl longs for her roots and the fundamental difference that would define

Figure 9.1. La Ciguapa and a little boy in a version of the Dominican folktale retold by Julia Álvarez, illustrated by Fabián Negrín (2000). Reprinted courtesy of the publisher, Random House.

her. In Julia Alvarez's version of the same myth (2000), the little Ciguapa girl cannot restrain her curiosity to know about humans, and the little boy she meets is equally intrigued by her mystery (see fig. 9.1). This longing to know the other, to embrace difference, and to reclaim the past is the defining trait of today's children literature from Central America and the Caribbean.

What ties the old and the new together, however, is neither a drive to entertain, nor teach, nor delight, nor transmit national identity and values, nor construct or deconstruct dominant ideologies or paradigms, though the works that have been considered here do all of these things. The common thread in over a century's worth of literature for children from Central America and the Caribbean is the un(adult)erated expression of hope. Why else would sophisticated writers turn their attention to children unless they shared the implicit faith that somehow, against all odds, children would understand them? In this seed of communication lies a kind of border interaction, a mingling of pluralities, in which differences reach out to one another. In this attempt to recognize the self and know the other that underpins the area's literature for children resides the hope for the creation of a world where all can be heard and none are silenced.

Notes

1. Introduction: Walking in Reverse/Reading in Reverse

1. See Ranajit Guha's definition of subalternity in his preface to *Selected Subaltern Studies* (35), "a name for the general attribute of subordination . . . whether this is expressed in terms of class, caste, *age*, gender and office or in any other way" (my emphasis); also note that postcolonial critics often compare children to colonial subjects, the object of the civilizing desire of adults, the colonizers: "good colonial subjects who might cause mischief and trouble, but who were educable" (Kutzer 140). Roderick McGillis, for example, states point blank: "Children are colonial subjects. Adults are the colonizers; children the colonized" (xxviii).

2. Julia L. Mickenberg's study does mention a kind of subversive children's literature that appeared in the United States during the McCarthy era written by political progressives (see Mickenberg).

3. Octavio Paz analyzed this phenomenon of refusing to "rajar" [break down or tear] in Mexican culture in his seminal work *El Laberinto de la soledad* (1950). Except where specified, all translations from Spanish to English are my own.

4. See "Children's Literature and Prestige" (Lathey 18–19). "The outcry over popular titles like *Are you There God? It's Me, Margaret* (in the 1970s) or, more recently, over the Harry Potter books obscures the fact that most children's books tend to receive very little attention, critical or otherwise" (Mickenberg 14).

5. See Anderson's study on the national imaginary, also, the studies by Sommer, Bhabha and González Echevarría that deconstruct the fictions of national identity and national liberation struggles. This disintegration of the concept of the nation also forms part of the Foundational Statement of the Latin American Subaltern Studies Group: "the deterritorialization of the nation-state under the impact of the new permeability of frontiers to capital-labor flows merely replicates, in effect, the genetic process of implantation of a colonial economy in Latin America. . . . It is not only that we can *no longer* operate solely within the prototype of nationhood; the concept of the nation, itself tied to the protagonism of Creole elites concerned to dominate and/or manage other social groups and classes in their own societies, has obscured, *from the start*, the presence of subaltern social subjects in Latin American history" (qtd. in Beverley 7; italics in the original).

6. See, for example, studies of African literature (Khorana).

7. These terms are not interchangeable. Hybrid forms are those elements of native culture that are interjected in altered form into hegemonic culture, mixed, if you will, though not blended. The best examples I have seen lately are the McDonald's in Costa Rica. A typical Costa Rican dish "gallo pinto," a unique mixture of rice and black beans that is associated exclusively with Costa Rica, is offered at the local McDonald's as "McPinto." Syncretic forms, on the other hand, are those elements that maintain a certain cultural integrity and refuse to be erased, existing alongside hegemonic practices—Costa Rican marimba music at a party, for example, followed up by karaoke.

8. Cf. Pope Benedict XVI's remark in Brazil (May 2007) denying that Catholicism was imposed on the indigenous populations, but that they had "longed for it in silence."

2. In the Beginning: José Martí and *La edad de oro*

1. Manuel Maldonado Denis even goes so far as to compare Martí to Franz Fanon, the preeminent Martinican who fought for the decolonization of his adopted African homeland, Algeria, and who described the psychopathology of colonialism in his *The Wretched of the Earth*: "He aquí un hombre que desde casi un siglo antes que el siquiatra martiniqués, ya había diagnosticado los males ínsitos al coloniaje y había captado con tanta claridad los futuros designios imperialistas de los pujantes Estados Unidos" (190) [Here is a man who, almost a century before the Martinican psychiatrist, had already diagnosed the inherent ills of colonialism and had captured with such clarity the future imperialistic designs of the burgeoning United States].

2. Critics in Martí's own day were surprised at the artistic level of *La edad de oro*, which they feared would be of inferior quality because it was aimed at child readers. See Lolo's thorough introduction to the historical and critical background of *La edad de oro*: "El hecho de que un famoso escritor para adultos emprendiera, aparentemente sin antecedente anterior en su obra, la tarea de escribir profesionalmente para los niños, fue algo que sorprendió a muchos—sino a todos—, particularmente porque entonces dicha categoría literaria era considerada, en la práctica, subliteratura" (*Mar de espuma* 16) [The fact that a famous writer for adults would take on, apparently without precedent in his previous work, the task of writing professionally for children, was something that surprised many—if not all—particularly because this category at that time was considered, in practice, a sub-literature].

3. Fraser claims that while "children's literature is an unlikely medium for social change" (223), arguing that most children's literature, even in Latin America, teaches children to value the dominant ideology, *La edad de oro* "maps

out what might be perceived as a subversive ideology for the youth of Cuba, and by extension for young people throughout the Americas."

4. For a thorough analysis of the publishing history of *La edad de oro* see Lolo (*Mar de espuma*), who argues that Da Costa may have been Jewish, which further complicates the issue.

5. His book of poems about a father and son, *Ismaelillo* (1882), is sometimes considered children's literature, but it was never directed specifically at children as was *La edad de oro*.

6. Hernández-Miyares renders Aristotle's advice as, "'*ilustrar deleitando*,' ser atractivo e interesante para los niños, instruirlos a la vez que brindarles consejo atinado, buen ejemplo y siempre alguna lección ética o moralizante que extraerán de la lectura" (17; italics his) ['*to illustrate pleasingly*,' to be attractive and interesting for children, to instruct them at the same time as provide them with well founded advice, good example, and always some ethical or moral lesson that they will extract from the reading].

7. For a study of Martí's essay on the *Iliad*, see Cancela.

8. There is some discussion as to whether María was his biological child or not; in any case, he was very close to her and helped bring her up (see Lolo "José Martí").

9. Had the magazine continued after the first four issues, Martí may indeed have dialogued with his readers since he had requested that they write him with their questions and comments and promised to publish some of their letters with his responses. Indeed, the final issue mentions that Martí has begun to receive letters from his readers, and in response to their questions about the veracity of his article on the Paris Exposition, he comments on the importance of telling the truth to children and includes an engraving "un grabado" of the Hall of Machines from the World Fair. See "A los niños que lean *La edad de oro*"; also "La última página" of the fourth issue.

10. Various critics have noted the implicit theme or intention of the story: "Martí ha sabido diluir sabiamente sus ideas antirracistas, sin hacerlas explícitas" (Pozo Campos 130) [Martí has wisely been able to dissolve his antiracist ideas (into the story) without making them explicit]; also "se esconde la moraleja nunca mentada de este relato de índole ejemplar sobre el prejuicio racial" (Klein 376) [the never mentioned moral hides in this story as a kind of exemplary model about racial prejudice].

11. Pozo Campos notes that "La caracterización de Raúl está dada por contraste; sus rasgos se hallan sugeridos, mediante la negación, la carencia de los de Bebé" (121) [Raúl's characterization is provided by contrast: his traits are suggested through negation, the absence of those of Bebé].

12. Pérez comments on the racial situation in Cuba at the time that Martí was writing: "Back then in Cuba, blacks and whites interacted on a personal level unthinkable in the United States. Nevertheless, there was a thin line that could not be trespassed, at least ideologically. It was a line that was supposed to show,

when so many walls of separation and discrimination had fallen, that there was still something that made blacks different, less equal; a line to convince even the most liberal minded that some walls should be preserved" (20).

13. Jiménez agrees with this assessment: "Para una búsqueda a la explicación de los postulados de Martí, vale mencionar que sus lecturas y su escritura se relacionan estrechamente a la corriente del conocimiento científico que permea históricamente la cultura occidental durante el siglo diecinueve" (251) [To find an explanation for Martí's beliefs, it is worth mentioning that his reading and writing are closely related to the current of scientific knowledge that historically permeated Western culture during the nineteenth century]. Cerezal, referring specifically to his pedagogical orientation, claims: "Martí . . . se suma a las corrientes renovadoras y progresistas de la educación del último tercio del siglo XIX" (65) [Martí is part of the renovating and progressive currents in education from the last third of the nineteenth century].

14. Fraser apparently disagrees, preferring to translate her name as "piety" and claiming that: "She embodies the 'piety' required for her struggle of liberation from externally imposed doctrines" (229).

3. And They All Lived Unhappily Ever After: Carmen Lyra and *Cuentos de mi tiá Panchita*

1. See González and Sáenz. For a more recent evaluation see Rojas and Ovares.

2. See Swain.

3. See Wilkins.

4. See Araujo Aguilar et al. and Víquez Guzmán.

5. See Barquero Arias, Madrigal Abarca, and González Araya.

6. "La cucarachita Mandinga."

7. For a review of her criticism, see chapter one of Víquez Guzmán. Also see Quesada Soto *Uno y los otros*, for a more recent evaluation of her work.

8. Rojas and Ovares claim that "aparecen en los cuentos de tío Conejo y tío Coyote personajes ligados a la tradición indígena del continente" (81) [in the stories of uncle Rabbit and uncle Coyote, characters appear who are linked to the indigenous tradition of the continent].

9. See Castro Rawson. Also note that Lyra has been labeled a realist, a naturalist, a romantic, and an idealist by her various critics. There are two reasons for such confusion: one, these European literary currents were influential in Latin America concurrently, not sequentially, and second, her novels for adults reflect a very different tone from that of her stories for children.

10. See Chase, who claims she is the first Costa Rican writer to transcend "*el costumbrismo*" and French style realism to try to write social realism (11).

11. See Molina Jiménez *Tía Panchita*, for documentation from the U.S. National Archives as to how Carmen Lyra's political activities were watched and reported by U.S. intelligence from 1932–1944.

12. See González Araya who excludes Lyra's children's stories from her study of Lyra's political views in her essays since *Cuentos de mi tía Panchita* represents "su dimensión más conocida—y menos peligrosa, además" (10) [her best-known—and least dangerous—dimension].

13. Lyra was writing at a time when all of Latin America was trying to invent a new identity ("Nuestra América" as Martí advocated), and within this continental imaginary, nation states were consolidating and emphasizing national characteristics, reflected and encouraged in literature through *costumbrismo* movements, social realism, and the political essay. See Chanady for a variety of approaches to the issue of national identity formation and Quesada Soto "Nación y enajenación" for a study of identity formation specifically in Costa Rican letters. He places Lyra in the second wave of Costa Rican novelists "la segunda promoción" who, most notably, begin to decenter the imagined identity promoted by the first wave of Creole elites linked to agricultural production for the international market.

14. Rojas and Ovares agree that "el lector costarricense siente una cercanía con estos cuentos" (81) [the Costa Rican reader feels a closeness to these tales] but attribute the feeling to the language she uses and the everyday objects she includes.

15. See Amoretti, p. 63.

16. Certainly the black population, even more marginalized than the Creole whites, felt the need to teach children to see themselves as astute. See Duncan and Meléndez: "Por medio de sus fábulas, el negro le enseñó a sus hijos—acaso inconscientemente—que la astucia es una virtud si se es negro y se vive en una sociedad racista, blanca y opresora" (140) [Through fables, the black taught his children—perhaps unconsciously—that astuteness is a virtue if one is black and lives in a racist, white, oppressive society].

17. See discussion of Ferré in ch. 4 for an analysis of the Puerto Rican version.

18. Quesada Pacheco, p. 236.

19. See Mignolo's *The Idea of Latin America* for an explanation of how the theology of the sixteenth and seventeenth centuries moved into ego-logy after the Industrial Revolution.

20. The diminutive "illo" is ambiguous in Costa Rica. It tends to be somewhat pejorative and paternalistic in that it indicates someone larger (the adult) looking fondly down on someone or something smaller (a child [un chiquillo], for example).

21. See Margarita Dobles, for example.

22. On a visit in 2007 to some Costa Rican bookstores, I found no fewer than four different editions/printings of Lyra's *Cuentos de mi tía Panchita*.

4. A Question of Power: Rosario Ferré and *Sonatinas*

1. See Fernández Olmos, "Constructing Heroines" and "Los cuentos," Palmer-López, and Morrison.

2. One study from 1999 claims to cover the entire section of six stories in the section "Cuentos Maravillos" in *Sonatinas*, but actually gives only an extended analysis of "Arroz con leche" and "Pico Rico Mandorico" (Palmer-López).

3. See Efraín Barradas and Andrés Candelario in Hintz, "An Annotated Bibliography" 649. Note also that both reviewers are male and, therefore, may have a stake in labeling Ferré's work subversive.

4. This study is not the place to investigate the multiple definitions of children's literature or to determine what is or is not suitable for children. For my purposes, any work that is designated for children either by the author, the publisher, the schools, the parents, or any other source in a position to allocate values qualifies as children's literature. Neither complexity nor subversion is a disqualifying attribute; rather they make children's stories even more interesting. As Ferré herself explains in her introduction to *Sonatinas*, "Como toda obra de arte, el cuento de hadas puede tener multiples significados" (10) [Like all works of art, the fairy tale can have multiple meanings]. Just as stories can have multiple meanings, they can also have multiple audiences. It is not uncommon for children's stories to say one thing to the child and something else to the parent reading the story aloud to the child.

5. A status that postcolonial critics, following Antonio Gramsci, label the subaltern.

6. Her decision to support statehood is predicated on the condition that Puerto Rico maintain its language and spearhead the effort to improve human rights for the Hispanic population in general in the United States. See Ferré's interview with Toral Alemañ.

7. It is interesting that of the three tales Ferré claims are not transcriptions or inscriptions of stories she has heard but products of her own imagination, this story has been completely ignored by her critics as opposed to the other two, which have generated several studies.

8. Ferré uses the symbol of the monkey in her adult fiction as well, specifically in "El cuento envenenado" where she inserts the popular expression "la mona, aunque la visten de seda, mona se queda" (*Papeles de Pandora* 231) [the monkey, even if you dress her in silk, is still a monkey]. She refers here to the claim that people from the lower class, no matter how much money they might have, can never become part of the upper class since they are separated by more than mere social barriers; they are ontologically different.

9. Doris M. Vazquez, "Rosario Ferré: Una cuentista puertorriquéna (sic) contemporánea" (*A Contemporary Puerto Rican Storyteller*). Yale–New Haven Teachers Institute. March 18, 2007. http://www.yale.edu/ynhti/curriculum/units/1987/1/87.01.09.x.html

10. "Rosario Ferré is one of a group of angry young Puerto Rican women authors who have seized the pen and wielded it effectively" (Glenn 207).

5. The Debate Over Racism: Joaquín Gutiérrez and *Cocorí*

1. See Gólcher "Leer *Cocorí*"; also Pérez-Yglesias, "Polémica y espectáculo" 53.

2. Gutiérrez's manuscript won the Rapa Nuí prize for best children's novel in Chile in 1947.

3. See Duncan; also Duncan and Powell. Powell wrote her graduate thesis on this topic in 1985.

4. See Joaquín Gutiérrez, "Cocorí es mi hijo menor" and Muñoz, "El papá de Cocorí."

5. Gutiérrez, "El racismo y el espejo." Also see Santos Pasamontes who quotes Gutiérrez in 1984 as insisting that in *Cocorí* "hay un contenido filosófico, político y cultural, contra los malos duraderos frente a los buenos frágiles, perecederos" [there is a philosophical, political and cultural content against abiding evil in the face of fragil, perishable good].

6. These exams were discontinued in 2007.

7. See Mondol (44) who discusses the court decision.

8. See Campbell's reaction to public protest over removing *Cocorí* from school reading lists: "No es con emotividad, con exageraciones que rayan en lo fantasioso, sin información, con descalificaciones previas, con irrespeto y sin razones como se debate y se construye. Respeto, exijo respeto" [It is not with emotional arguments, with exaggerations that border on the fantastic, without information and with previous disqualifications, with disrespect and without reasons that one debates and constructs. Respect, I demand respect].

9. See Pacheco, who explains publicly why he took this measure despite his belief that Gutiérrez is one of the nation's best writers.

10. See Fabiola Martínez for a range of reactions, both in favor and against removing the novel from required reading lists. Fabiola Martínez quotes children's literature professor and author Carlos Rubio as saying "Ningúna lectura obligatoria puede ser atractiva para los estudiantes" (6) [No obligatory reading can be attractive for students]. Also see Rubio "Cocorí."

11. See articles and editorials that appeared in Costa Rica's leading newspapers *La Nación* and *La República* during the months of April and May 2003 with titles such as "Matar a un ruiseñor" [To kill a mockingbird], "¿Por qué expulsaron a Cocorí?" [Why did they expel Cocorí?], "La falacia de una literatura pura" [The fallacy of pure literature], "Racismo en la mente" [Racism in the mind], "Cocorí y sus adversarios" [Cocorí and his adversaries], "¿*Cocorí* racista?" [*Cocorí* racist?]. Also see Valembois.

12. The School of Philology, Linguistics, and Literature at the University of Costa Rica had been planning a colloquium on Gutiérrez prior to the outbreak

of the public debate. Because of the controversy, the conference transformed, according to its Coordinator Dr. Jorge Chen Sham, "en un acto reivindicatorio de su legado literario y una defensa de su novela infantil *Cocorí*" [into a vindication of Gutiérrez's literary legacy and a defense of his novel for children *Cocorí*], May 29–30, 2003. A special edition of the journal *Káñina*, Vol. 28 (2004) published the proceedings from this conference.

13. See Ramírez; also the back cover of the 1995 edition.

14. See Pineda Lima for a complete bibliography.

15. See Arias Formoso; Iraheta; Ramos, Cañas; and "Cocorí, un cuento inolvidable."

16. Studies range from early analyses of Gutiérrez's narrative in 1957 (Schade) to a specific analysis of style in *Cocorí* in 1969 (Vargas) and narrative structure in 1983 (Pérez-Yglesias) to two fairly recent studies—one, which looks at the moral lessons learned by Cocorí (wisdom, goodness, worthiness, justice, and solidarity) (Oviedo 1993), and the other that analyzes the classical rhetorical structure of the novel (Sparisci Lovicelli, "Lectura Retórica"). None of these essays even so much as mentions the issue of racism. Nevertheless, a special edition of *Káñina* appeared in 2004 devoted to Gutiérrez's work with a majority of the articles dealing in one form or another with the polemic.

17. This edition was reprinted consistently every one to two years through 2003 (Pineda Lima 92–93).

18. Gólcher, in her newspaper article "Leer *Cocorí*" quotes his widow Elena Nascimento as saying, "Para Joaquín, Limón siempre fue lo máximo. Él tenía un gran respeto y cariño por los negros, jamás habría alguna intención racista" [For Joaquín, Limón was always wonderful. He had great respect and cared deeply for the blacks; there never was any racist intention].

19. See his defense of *Cocorí* in "El racismo y un espejo."

20. See interview with Andricaín Hernández. Gutiérrez's answer to the question about why he chose the name Cocorí "Para rendirle homenaje a un cacique nuestro que se enfrentó a los conquistadores españoles. Se llamaba Cocorí y su tribu se defendió valientemente de los invasores" [To pay homage to one of our chiefs who faced the Spanish conquistadors. His name was Cocorí and his tribe defended themselves valiantly against the invaders]. For more on the Amerindian *cacique* Cocorí and the significance of his name in relation to Gutiérrez's novel, see Robles Mohs.

21. See Quesada Soto for an explanation of the process of Costa Rican identity formation from 1890–1940.

22. On this point, I disagree with Caamaño Morúa's argument that Gutiérrez's emphasis on the color black "acentúa su exotismo, su 'otredad'" ("*Cocorí*" 30) [emphasizes his exoticism, his "otherness"].

23. See Rubio: "todos los que leímos a *Cocorí* de niños nos sentimos biografiados en el texto" ("Cocorí" 69) [all of us who read *Cocorí* as children felt ourselves "biographied" in the text].

24. One Web site on Costa Rica calls him "Costa Rica's Huckleberry Finn." Feb. 14, 2007. http://www.centralamerica.com/cr/moon/moart.htm

25. "A breve vida nace destinada,/ sus edades son horas en un día" "Soneto ofreciendo a Velisa la primera Rosa que abrió el Verano" [It is born destined to a brief life/ its ages are hours in a day. Sonnet offering to Velisa the first Rose of Summer].

26. See Chen Sham, who calls this cultural text "Cronotopo de Indias, el texto de descubrimiento/conquista, el cual reproduce el encuentro entre el hombre blanco (europeo) y el otro subalterno nativo, llámase indio, asiático o negro" (35) [Chronotope of the Indies, the text of discovery/conquest, which reproduces the meeting between the white (European) man and the other subaltern native, whether he be called Indian, Asian, or Negro]. See also Rodríguez Jiménez, who reminds us that *Cocorí* was written barely two years after the end of World War II: "Estados Unidos se eregía (sic) como una potencia indiscutible del planeta" (58) [The United States arose as an unarguable power on the planet].

27. All quotations from *Cocorí* are taken from the 1995 edition and are identified by page number in parenthesis.

28. Robles Mohs also claims that the monkey is a symbol of the artist in several Mesoamerican indigenous cultures (65).

29. We should remember that Cocorí's name is neither African nor Creole, but indigenous. Like the Amerindians, he gives gifts that are valuable for him.

30. It is odd that other critics, even those who discuss this initial gift giving scene (Chen Sham; Robles Mohs), never mention Cocorí's stories/art as one of the gifts that the New World has tried to give to the Old.

31. The collection originated in the Middle East in the fifteenth century but was appropriated by the West through French translation in the eighteenth century.

32. Rodríguez Jiménez reminds us that Costa Rica's national flower is the orchid (58).

33. In earlier editions of the book, the little girl mistakes Cocorí for a monkey, but given the lawsuit against the book, Gutiérrez obviously realized that this scene was too controversial and eliminated the reference in subsequent editions. See Chen Sham's article for a defense of this scene and a critique of Gutiérrez's revision.

34. Chen Sham is correct here in pointing out the difference between the authentic and equal exchange in the children's gift giving scene versus that of Columbus's gifts of worthless trinkets that he reports in his letter of October 12, 1492 (35).

35. Sparisci Lovicelli (2004) notes the symmetry between the "*locus amoenus y locus eremus*, marcos ideales para reflejar la aproximación o el alejamiento de la meta de Cocorí: la satisfacción de su *curiositas*" (73) [*locus amoenus* and *locus oremus*, ideal frames to reflect the approximation or distance from Cocorí's goal: the satisfaction of his *curiositas*].

36. For more about the classical origin of this paradox, see Brenes Morales.

37. It is significant that the jungle snake has eaten an entire bull leaving only his horns sticking out of the snake's mouth. The image of the devil is unmistakable, although Argüello Scriba, interprets the snake with horns as a dragon (18). I am indebted to my colleague Maryrica Lottman for the reminder that the bull is the traditional symbol of Spain. The fact that the tropical snake eats the bull, thus, suggests an even more intriguing response to colonialism.

38. See Cartín de Guier. Part of the problem with her defense of *Cocorí* is her conflation of "universal culture" with Western culture: "La obra de Joaquín Gutiérrez está inserta en la cultura universal" [The work of Joaquín Gutiérrez is inserted into universal culture] and "dentro de la tradición de la cultura universal, la verdad está en el arte" [within the tradition of universal culture, truth is in art]. See also Sparisci Lovicelli.

39. Rodríguez Jiménez argues for the text's ambivalence on other grounds using Julia Kristeva's theoretical explanations concerning the fundamental ambivalence of all novels "precisamente porque es una novela" (56–57) [precisely because it is a novel].

40. Significantly, mama Drusila, despite her initial condescension toward the Negro Cantor "no me vengas con majaderías en verso" (58) [don't come to me with your stupid verses], consults him as a last resort to find Cocorí who has been missing for two days. Based on his vision of Cocorí approaching the snake, she fears the worst "casi segura de haber perdido para siempre a su Negrito, volvió hacia su casa con la cabeza baja. El dolor en su pecho, ardiente como una zarzamora, le arañaba todas las fibras de su alma" (59) [almost sure of having lost her little black boy, she returned toward her house with her head hanging. The pain in her chest, burning like a blackberry bush, scratched all the fibers of her soul].

6. Dissent from Within: Manlio Argueta's *Los perros mágicos de los volcanes*

1. Chosen as the fifth best Latin American novel by Modern Library's 2002 list of the 100 best Latin American novels. Still, Argueta maintains that he comes from the periphery of the periphery and, therefore, "doesn't command the attention of Latin American critics, as others do" (Milan Arias 2). All of Argueta's comments in this interview have been translated into English by Milan Arias.

2. Note that the use of this term in U.S. education bears no resemblance to the anthropological term (coined by Cuban Fernando Ortíz in 1940 and later applied to literary theory by Angel Rama in 1982), which implies various kinds of responses to "the imposition of European cultural and literary forms . . . in such a way as to create hybrid forms" (see Emery for a discussion of transculturation

in Latin American literature 10–14). Pratt and Beaty formulate their own definition by which they simply mean books from other countries (transcultural
works) as opposed to books from other cultures, subcultures or ethnic groups
from within the same country (multicultural works).

3. It should be remembered that Argueta began his literary career as a poet.

4. See Ranajit Guha's definition of subalternity in ch. 1, note 1 of this study.

5. According to Argueta himself, "I do this to reaffirm our own values, local
values, so as to know that we exist" (Milan Arias 3).

6. "(T)enemos en cuenta que el soldado proviene de la clase campesina. Está
matando a los mismos campesinos, el sector social del que proviene" (Z. Martínez
440) [Let's keep in mind that the soldiers come from the peasant class. They are
killing the very *campesinos*, the social sector from which they come]. Argueta uses
this paradox as the thematic basis for his novel *Cuzcatlán donde bate la mar del
sur* (1986).

7. According to Lurie, "The great subversive works of children's literature suggest that there are other views of human life besides those of the shopping mall
and the corporation. They mock current assumptions and express the imaginative, unconventional, noncommercial view of the world in its simplest and pur-
est form. They appeal to the imaginative, questioning, rebellious child within
all of us, renew our instinctive energy, and act as a *force for change*" (xi; my
emphasis).

8. See John Beverley's comments on Gayatri Spivak's thesis that the subaltern
cannot speak "in a way that would carry any sort of authority or meaning for us
without altering the relations of power/knowledge that constitute it as subaltern
in the first place" (29).

9. See Minh-ha's discussion of "the margins within the center and the centers
within the margin" (Ashcroft 216).

10. It is interesting from an anecdotal standpoint that the American mother
of one of my students from a recent children's literature class read this book by
Argueta and was totally baffled by it.

11. See Mignolo's *The Idea of Latin America*.

12. This line is not in the first edition, but Argueta plans to add it to the second edition. Personal communication with Linda Craft, January 12, 2007; translation mine.

7. Transgressing Limits: Gioconda Belli and *El taller de las mariposas*

1. Actually, one article refers to the work as part of her narrative corpus but
calls it a book of short stories, which it is not (López Astudillo 106). The entry
on Belli in Gale's *Dictionary of Literary Biography* (Preble-Niemi) dedicates two
sentences to the book and completely misrepresents the plot, claiming that the

story "tells of a laboratory worker who whimsically crosses a flower and an insect to create the butterfly." The entire point of the story is that the protagonist, who is not a laboratory worker but a designer in Belli's recreation of the cosmos, is not allowed to cross elements of the vegetable realm (a flower) with elements of the animal realm (an insect); and the animal in question is not an insect but a hummingbird. The point is that neither of these critics even bothered to read the story. Were they assuming, perhaps, that a child's book is neither relevant to nor worthy of comment in an overview of Belli's narrative corpus? The only critic I have been able to find who discusses this story surfaced almost by accident as I reviewed bibliography on Belli from the University of Costa Rica. I discovered an M.A. thesis written by a Costa Rican student that had a few pages devoted to Belli's story.

2. Rewriting the myth of creation is a recurrent theme in Belli's work since her early poems, *De la costilla de Eva* (1987).

3. Moyano is talking here about Belli's futuristic novel *Waslala* (written at the same time as Belli's children's book), which presents the loss of utopia and the future of Latin America as "grandes extensiones de tierra donde prevalecen las guerras y el narcotráfico, el caos en suma, y cuyo fin será el convertirse en el basurero de la tecnología y el progreso del Norte" [large extensions of land where wars and drug trafficking prevail, in sum chaos, and whose destiny is to become the trash heap for the technology and progress of the North].

4. Contrary to the case of *Cocorí* discussed in ch. 5, the illustrations seem well thought out and purposefully designed to convey imagery congruent with the messages of the text.

5. See Fayes, for example, who quotes Paula Gunn Allen in "The Sacred Hoop: A Contemporary Perspective," to explain that "indigenous peoples understand life as a 'sacred hoop,' which is 'the concept of a singular unity that is dynamic and encompassing, including all that is contained in its most essential aspect, that of life—that is, dynamic and aware, partaking as it does in the life of the All Spirit and contributing as it does to the continuing of life of that same Great Mystery.' An important consequence of these beliefs is that 'tribal people allow all animals, vegetables, and minerals (the entire biota, in short) the same or even greater privilege than humans' (243). This attitude toward nature is characteristic not only of North American Indian cultures but also of the indigenous peoples of Central America."

8. Politically Correct in Costa Rica: Lara Ríos, Leonardo Garnier, and Carlos Rubio

1. See for example Ana Cristina Rosetti's *La loca de Gandoca* and Fernando Contreras' *Única mirando el mar* for recent examples of ecological themes; Rosetti's *Limón Blues* about the Afro Caribbean community and Tatiana Lobo's

Assault on Paradise, a revision of the conquest narrative, to name only some of the most popular.

2. Chacón bases his argument on Edmond Cros: "la alteridad no es representable, puesto que la identificación con el otro no puede hacerse más que a través de mis propios modelos discursivos que, a su vez, han sido producidos para expresar lo que yo sé, lo que yo soy o lo que imagino ser, y no han sido producidos más que para eso; de ahí su incapacidad para dar cuenta de lo que está fuera de mí y de mi universo" (qtd. in Chacón) [Alterity cannot be represented since the identification with the other cannot happen outside of my own discursive models, which, at the same time, have been produced to express what I know, what I am or what I imagine myself to be, and they have not been produced for anything other than that; hence their incapacity to recognize what is outside of me or outside of my universe].

3. See two articles by Jean Franco along these lines "¿La historia de quién? La piratería postmoderna" and "*Si me permiten hablar*: La lucha por el poder interpretativo."

4. As Garnier reminded me in an interview in July 2007, "After all, the monkey studied in France. He is not just providing cheap labor."

5. The key here is *fair* trade as opposed to *free* trade—arguments for and against passage of the Central American Free Trade Act (CAFTA or TLC—Tratado de Libre Comercio) notwithstanding. Fair trade assumes that there is a level playing field in terms of resources, products and services, power and influence. Free is just that, no rules, restrictions, tariffs or handicaps placed on the more powerful, longer established, North American markets in their dealings with the much smaller and economically impoverished countries of Central America. What Garnier glosses over, however, is everything that Costa Rica stands to lose in this artificially equal association of the weak with the powerful, specifically, its autonomy.

6. For reviews see Andricaín Hernández and Rodríguez.

7. For reviews see Céspedes and Méndez Garita.

8. See Caamaño Morúa and Méndez Garita.

9. <http://www.carlosrubioescritor.com>

10. For reviews see Andricaín Hernández, Rodríguez, and C. Sánchez.

11. For a critical review see Morera Salas.

9. Conclusion: Juan Bobo's True IQ

1. See for example Ricardo Alegría's collection of *Cuentos folklóricos de Puerto Rico* that includes several Juan Bobo stories, including one in which the foolish figure is renamed Pedro Animala, as is one from the Ferré collection. In general, however, both collections portray a man who is not as foolish as he seems.

Bibliography

Alegría, Ricardo E. *Cuentos folklóricos de Puerto Rico*. San Juan: Colección de Estudios Puertorriqueños, 2002.

Alvarez, Julia. *The Secret Footprints*. New York: Alfred A. Knopf, 2000.

Amoretti, Maria. *Debajo del canto: Un análisis del Himno Nacional de Costa Rica*. San José, Costa Rica: Editorial de la Universidad de Costa Rica, 1987.

Anderson, Benedict. *Imagined Communities*, rev. ed. 1983. London: Verso, 1991.

Anderson, Danny J., and Jill Kuhnheim. *Cultural Studies in the Curriculum: Teaching Latin America*. New York: The Modern Language Association of America, 2003.

Andricaín Hernández, Sergio. "La voz de Cocorí." *La Nación* 5 July 1992.

———. "Un cuento de hadas a las puertas del tercer milenio." *Revista Latinoamericana de Literatura Infantil y Juvenil* 5 (1997). 10 May 2007 <http://www.carlosrubioescritor.com/joomla/index.php?option=com_content&task=view&id=42&Itemid=58>.

Andricaín Hernández, Sergio, and Antonio Orlando Rodríguez. "Review of Pedro y su teatrino maravilloso." 10 May 2007 <http://www.carlosrubioescritor.com/joomla/index.php?option=com_content&task=view&id=41&Itemid=57>.

Araujo Aguilar, Patricia, et al. "Rasgos comunes de tres categorías de análisis en el relato literario." Licenciatura Thesis. University of Costa Rica, 1977.

Argüello Scriba, Sol. "La simbología de los animales en *Cocorí*." *Káñina* 28. Número especial. (2004): 11–20.

Argueta, Manlio. *El Cipitío*. Trans. Linda Craft. San José, Costa Rica: Editorial Legado, 2006.

———. *El siglo de o(g)ro*. San Salvador: Dirección de Publicaciones e Impresos, 1997.

———. *Magic Dogs of the Volcanoes/Los perros mágicos de los volcanes*. Trans. Stacey Ross. San Francisco: Children's Book Press, 1990.

Arias, Arturo. *Gestos ceremoniales*. Guatemala: Impresos Industriales, S.A., 1998.

———. *Taking Their Word: Literature and the Signs of Central America*. Minneapolis: University of Minnesota Press, 2007.

Arias Formoso, Rodolfo, comp. *Retrato de Joaquín Gutiérrez*. San José, Costa Rica: Editorial de la Universidad de Costa Rica, 2002.

Arias, Santa, and Mariselle Meléndez, eds. *Mapping Colonial Spanish America: Places and Commonplaces of Identity, Culture, and Experience.* Lewisburg, PA: Bucknell University Press, 2002.

Armas, Daniel. *Prontuario de literatura infantil.* Guatemala: HR Impresores, S.A., 2003.

Ashcroft, Bill, Gareth Griffiths, and Helen Tiffin, eds. *The Post-Colonial Studies Reader.* London: Routledge, 1995.

Barquero Arias, Rosa María. "La focalización en *Los otros cuentos de Carmen Lyra*." Licenciatura Thesis. University of Costa Rica, 1996.

Barthes, Roland. *The Pleasure of the Text.* Trans. Richard Miller. New York: Hill and Wang, 1973.

Bearne, Eve, and Victor Watson, eds. *Where Texts and Children Meet.* London: Routledge, 2000.

Belli, Gioconda. *De la costilla de Eva.* Managua: Editorial Nueva Nicaragua, 1987.

———. *El taller de las mariposas.* Managua: Ananá Ediciones Centroamericanas, 1996.

Bermúdez, Manuel. "Cocorí o el anhelo de una rosa negra." *La Nación* 11 May 2003.

Bertrand Barbe, Norbert. "Modelización de las figuras del pensamiento Latinoamericano en la literatura nicaragüense: los orígenes prehispánicos e indígenos de las figuras y motivos en el Güegüence y las aventuras de Tío Coyote." 1 June 2007 <http://www.marcaacme.com/media/gueguenceymachos.pdf>.

Beverley, John. *Subalternity and Representation: Arguments in Cultural Theory.* Durham: Duke University Press, 1999.

Beverley, John, José Oviedo, and Michael Aronna. *The Postmodernism Debate in Latin America.* Durham: Duke University Press, 1995.

Bhabha, Homi, ed. *Nation and Narration.* London: Routledge, 1990.

Binder, Wolfgang. "Entrevista con Rosario Ferré." *La Torre: Revista General de la Universidad de Puerto Rico* 8.30 (1994): 239–253.

Blanco, Patricia. "Vidas de transgresión: Entrevista con Carlos Rubio." *Libros* 4.16 (2003). 10 May 2007 <http://www.carlosrubioescritor.com/joomla/index.php?option=com_content&task=view&id=22&Itemid=51>.

Blanco Díaz, Andrés. *La ciguapa, el pícaro y la dama: Relatos y leyendas dominicanos.* Mexico: Alfaguara Grupo Santillana, 2003.

Bosch, Juan. *Con Indios: Apuntes históricos y leyendas.* Ciudad Trujillo, Dominican Republic: Editorial La Nación, 1935.

Brenes Morales, Jorge. "Fábula y paradoja en *Cocorí*." *Káñina* 28. Número especial. (2004): 21–26.

Caamaño Morúa, Virginia. "*Cocorí*: una lectura desde la perspectiva de la construcción identitaria costarricense." *Káñina* 28. Número especial. (2004): 27–32.

———. "La mujer que se sabía todos los cuentos . . . pero no sabía su nombre." Paper presented 25 September 2003. Instituto de México: San José, Costa Rica. 10 May 2007 <http://www.carlosrubioescritor.com/joomla/index. php?option=com_content&task=view&id=34&Itemid=48>.

Campbell, Epsy. "*Cocorí*: Una larga lucha en contra de los estereotipos y el racismo." *La República* 1 May 2003.

Cancela, Miranda. "Leyendo en *La edad de oro*: 'La Ilíada de Homero.'" *La Universidad de La Habana* 240 (1991): 39–53.

Cantillano, Odilie Alicia. "Carmen Lira y 'Los cuentos de mi tía Panchita': Aspectos folklóricos, literarios y lingüísticos." Diss. University of Arizona, 1972.

Cañas, Albert F. "Chisporroteos." *La República* 5 December 1971.

Cartín de Guier, Estrella. "Enhorabuena, Cocorí." *La Nación* 15 August 2003.

Castegnaro, Ernesto. "El día histórico." *La Nación* 27 August 1973: 15.

Castro Rawson, Margarita. *El costumbrismo en Costa Rica*. San José: Editorial Costa Rica, 1966.

Cerezal, Fernando. "'Enseñar con ternura y sabiduría': Las concepciones pedagógicas de José Martí." *CIEFL Bulletin* 7.1–2 (1996): 59–76.

Certau, Michel de. *Practices of Everyday Life*. Berkeley and Los Angeles: University of California Press, 1984.

Céspedes, Edgar. "Review of *El libro de la Navidad*." *La Nación* 25 December 2001. 10 May 2007 <http://www.carlosrubioescritor.com/joomla/index .php?option=com_content&task=view&id=37&Itemid=53>.

Chacón Gutiérrez, Albino. "La oralidad y su reescritura literaria." *Estudios Hispánicos en la Red*. 2005. 10 May 2007 <http://artsandscience1.concordia .ca/cmll/spanish/antonio/chacon.ht>.

Chanady, Amaryll, ed. *Latin American Identity and Constructions of Difference*. Minneapolis: University of Minnesota Press, 1994.

Chase, Alfonso. Introduction: Carmen Lyra maestro y compañera. *Los otros cuentos de Carmen Lyra*, by Carmen Lyra. San José: Editorial Costa Rica, 1985. 7–13.

Chaves, María José. "La Alegoría como método en los cuentos y ensayos de Rosario Ferré." *Third Woman* 2.2 (1984): 64–76.

Chen Sham, Jorge. "El cronotopo de indias y el sujeto afro-caribeño: recepción de *Cocorí*." *Káñina* 28. Número especial. (2004): 33–40.

Chrisman, Laura, and Benita Parry, eds. *Postcolonial Theory and Criticism*. Cambridge: D.S. Brewer, 2000.

"La Ciguapa." 2 June 2007 <http://www.jmarcano.com/mipais/cultura/mitos/ ciguapa.html>.

Clark, Beverly Lyon. *Kiddie Lit: The Cultural Construction of Children's Literature in America*. Baltimore: The Johns Hopkins University Press, 2003.

Cliff, Michelle. *The Land of Look Behind*. Ithaca, NY: Firebrand Books, 1985.

Clifford, James, and George E. Marcus, eds. *Writing Culture: The Poetics and Politics of Ethnography*. Berkley: University of California Press, 1986.

"Cocorí, un cuento inolvidable." *La Nación* 9 September 1971.

"¿Cocorí racista?" *La Nación Revista Dominical* 20 April 2003: 15.

Cortés, Carlos. *La gran novela perdida: historia personal de la narrativa costarrisible*. San Jose, Costa Rica: Ediciones Perro Azul, 2007.

Craft, Linda J. "*Ex libris*: Childhood, Memory, and Literature in Manlio Argueta's *Siglo de o(g)ro*." *Antípodas* 10 (1998): 129–140.

Cruz, Jacqueline. "'Esclava vencedora': La mujer en la obra literaria de José Martí." *Hispania* 75.1 (1992): 30–37.

Del Sarto, Ana, Alicia Ríos, and Abril Trigo, eds. *The Latin American Cultural Studies Reader*. Durham: Duke University Press, 2004.

Dobles, Aurelia. "Gioconda Belli: Vocera de la emoción y la razón." *La Nación*. Suplemento Áncora. 18 February 2007: 6–7.

Dobles, Margarita. *Literatura infantil*. 3rd ed. San José, Costa Rica: EUNED, 2000.

Dobrin, Sidney I., and Kenneth B. Kidd, eds. *Wild Things: Children's Culture and Ecocriticism*. Detroit: Wayne State University Press, 2004.

Duncan, Quince. "Algunas asemetrías en la novela *Cocorí*." 7 January 2003 <http://www.clubdelibros.com/archicocoriquince.htm>.

Duncan, Quince, and Carlos Meléndez. *El negro en Costa Rica*. 11th ed. San José, Costa Rica: Editorial Costa Rica, 2005.

Duncan, Quince, and Lorein Powell. *Dos estudios sobre diáspora negra y racismo*. Heredia, Costa Rica: IDELA, 1987.

Dupont, Denise. "Creators and Critics: Rosario Ferré Writes the Golden Age." *Revista de Estudios Hispánicos* 38 (2004): 343–368.

Elizagaray, Alga Marina. *La literatura de la revolución cubana para niños y jóvenes*. La Habana: Editorial ORBE, 1979.

Emery, Amy Fass. *The Anthropological Imagination in Latin American Literature*. Columbia: University of Missouri Press, 1996.

Fayes, Helene. "The Revolutionary Empowerment of Nature in Belli's *The Inhabited Woman*." *Mosaic* 38.2 (2005): 95–111.

Fernández Carballo, Rodolfo. "Utopía y desencantos en la construcción de una comunidad imaginada: *Waslala memorial del futuro* de Gioconda Belli." MA thesis. University of Costa Rica, 2006.

Fernández Olmos, Margarita. "Constructing Heroines: Rosario Ferré's Cuentos Infantiles and Feminine Instruments of Change." *The Lion and the Unicorn: A Critical Journal of Children's Literature* 10 (1986): 83–94.

———. "Los cuentos infantiles de Rosario Ferré, o la fantasía emancipadora." *Revista de Crítica Literaria Latinoamericana* 14.27 (1988): 151–163.

Fernández Retamar, Roberto. "About My Writing on Martí's Work." *World Literature Today* 76.3–4 (2002): 17–23.

Ferré, Rosario. *El medio pollito*. Mexico: Alfaguara Grupo Santillana, 1996.
———. *La cucarachita Martina*. Río Piedras, Puerto Rico: Ediciones Huracán, 1990.
———. *Papeles de Pandora*. Mexico: J. Mortiz, 1990.
———. *Sonatinas*. Río Piedras, Puerto Rico: Ediciones Huracán, 1989.
———. "The Writer's Kitchen." Trans. Diana L. Vélez. *Feminist Studies* 12.2 (1986): 227–242.
Finazzo, Denise Ann. *All for the Children: Multicultural Essentials of Literature*. Albany: Delmar Publishers, 1997.
Foner, Philip S., ed. *José Martí: On Education*. Trans. Elinor Randall. New York: Monthly Review Press, 1979.
Fox, Dana L., and Kathy G. Short. *Stories Matter: The Complexity of Cultural Authenticity in Children's Literature*. Urbana: National Council of Teachers of English, 2003.
Franco, Jean. *The Decline and Fall of the Lettered City: Latin America in the Cold War*. Cambridge: Harvard University Press, 2002.
———. "¿La historia de quién? La piratería postmoderna." *Revista de crítica literaria latinoamericana* 33 (1991): 11–20.
———. "*Si me permiten hablar*: La lucha por el poder interpretativo." *Revista de Crítica Literaria Latinoamericana* 18.36 (1992): 109–116.
Fraser, Howard M. "*La edad de oro* and José Martí's Modernist Ideology." *Revista Interamericana de Bibliografía/Inter-American Review of Bibliography* 42.2 (1992): 223–232.
Fuentes, Carlos. *La nueva novela hispanoamericana*. Mexico: Cuadernos de Joaquín Mortíz, 1969.
Gallego Alfonso, Emilia. "Apuntes sobre la presencia de la magia en *La edad de oro*." *La Universidad de La Habana* 229 (1987): 165–171.
———. "Para un estudio comparativo entre las *Cartas a Elpidio* y *La edad de oro*." *La Universidad de la Habana* 235 (1989): 95–108.
García Canclini, Néstor. *Consumers and Citizens: Globalization and Multicultural Conflicts*. Minneapolis: University of Minnesota Press, 2001.
———. *Hybrid Cultures: Strategies for Entering and Leaving Modernity*. Trans. Christopher L. Chiappari, and Silvia L. López. Minneapolis: University of Minnesota Press, 1995.
Garg, Pulin K. "Keynote Address." *Proceedings of International Conference: Transience and Transitions in Organisations*. Volume I. India: Indian Society for Individual and Social Development, 1986.
Garnier, Leonardo. *Gracias a usted*. San José, Costa Rica: Ediciones Farben, 2005.
———. *Mono Congo y León Panzón*. San José, Costa Rica: Farben Grupo Editorial Norma, 2001.
———. Web page. 14 May 2007 <www.leonardogarnier.com>.

————. *El sastrecillo ¿valiente?* Mexico: CIDCLI, 2004.

Glenn, Kathleen M. "Text and Countertext in Rosario Ferré's 'Sleeping Beauty.'" *Studies in Short Fiction* 33 (1996): 207–18.

Gólcher B., Raquel. "Cocorí y sus adversarios." *La Nación* 27 April 2003: 16A.

————. "Leer 'Cocorí' no será obligatorio: Asociación Proyecto Caribe lo considera racista." *La Nación* 22 April 2003.

González, Ann B. "The Question of Race: Joaquín Gutiérrez and *Cocorí.*" *Caribe* 10.2 (2007–2008): 1–17.

————. "Costa Rican Identity and the Stories of Carment Lyra." *SECOLAS Annals* 52 (2008): 73–82.

————. "Transgressing Limits: Belli's *El taller de las mariposas.*" *Ciberletras* 17 (Spring 2007).

González, Luisa, and Carlos Luis Sáenz. *Carmen Lyra.* San José, Costa Rica: Ministerio de Cultura, Juventud y Deportes, 1972; 2nd ed. San José, Costa Rica: Editorial Universidad Estatal a Distancia, 1998.

González Araya, María Nidia. "Carmen Lyra: Una voz acallada." MA thesis. University of Costa Rica, 1996.

González Echevarría, Roberto. *Myth and Archive: Towards a Theory of Latin American Narrative.* Cambridge: Cambridge University Press, 1990.

Guha, Ranajit, and Gayatri Spivak. *Selected Subaltern Studies.* New York: Oxford University Press, 1988.

Gutiérrez, Joaquín. *Cocorí.* Santiago de Chile: Editorial Rapa-Nui, S.A., 1947; 2nd. ed. San José, Costa Rica: Editorial Costa Rica, 1995.

————. *Cocorí.* Trans. Daniel McBain and illustrated Shawn Steffler. Dunvegan, Ont.: Cormorant Books, 1989.

————. "Cocorí es mi hijo menor." *Periódico Universidad* 8 July 1974.

————. "El racismo y un espejo." *Periódico Universidad* 14 October 1983.

Harris, Violet, ed. *Using Multiethnic Literature in the K–8 Classroom.* Norwood, Massachusetts: Christopher-Gordon Publishers, Inc., 1997.

Heneghan, Bridget T. *Whitewashing America: Material Culture and Race in the Antebellum Imagination.* Jackson: University Press of Mississippi, 2003.

Hernández Biosca, Roberto I. "*La edad de oro,* un contemporáneo." *La Universidad de la Habana* 235 (1989): 109–118.

Hernández-Miyares, Julio E. "José Martí y los cuentos de *La edad de oro.*" *La Nuez* 3 (1991): 17–19.

Hintz, Suzanne S. "An Annotated Bibliography of Works by and about Rosario Ferré: The First Twenty Years, 1970–1990." *Revista Interamericana de Bibliografía/Interamerican Review of Bibliography* 41.4 (1991): 643–54.

————. "La palabra, según Rosario Ferré." Proyecto Ensayo Hispánico. 20 December 2008 <http://www.ensayistas.org/filosofos/puertorico/ferre/introd.htm>.

Horan, Elizabeth Rosa. *The Subversive Voice of Carmen Lyra: Selected Works.* Gainesville: University Press of Florida, 2000.

Hourihan, Margery. *Deconstructing the Hero: Literary Theory and Children's Literature*. London: Routledge, 1997.

Iraheta, Ernesto. "Cocorí." *Diario de Costa Rica* 20 August 1971.

Izquierdo Miller, Inés. "José Martí y su vocación pedagógica." *Espéculo* 23 (2003). 15 March 2007 <http://www.ucm.es/info/especulo/numero23/marti_pe.html>.

Jiménez, Luis A. "José Martí, Darwin y el comportamiento de los animales en *La edad de oro*." *Ometeca* 3–4 (1996): 60–69.

Khorana, Meena, ed. *Critical Perspectives on Postcolonial African Children's and Young Adult Literature*. Westport, CT: Greenwood Press, 1998.

Klein, L. B. "Ficción y Magisterio en la narrativa de José Martí: 'La Muñeca Negra.'" *Quaderni Ibero-Americani: Actualita Culturale della Penisola Iberica e America Latina* 47–48 (1975–1976): 372–77.

Kutzer, M. Daphne. *Empire's Children: Empire and Imperialism in Classic British Children's Books*. New York: Garland Publishing, Inc., 2000.

Langer de Ramírez, Lori. *Cuéntame: Folklore y fábulas*. New York: Amsco School Publications, Inc., 1999.

Larrea, Elba. "La prosa de José Martí en *La edad de oro*." *Cuadernos del Congreso para la Libertad de la Cultura* 61 (1962): 3–10.

Lastra, Sarai. "Juan Bobo: A Folkloric Information System—how the controversial work of anthropologist J. Alden Mason, who collected Puerto Rican folklore, underscores the problem of authenticating folklore artifacts." *Library Trends* (1999). 1 June 2007 <http://findarticles.com/p/articles/mi_m1387/is_3_47/ai_54836351>.

Lathey, Gillian, ed. *The Translation of Children's Literature: A Reader*. Clevedon: Multilingual Matters LTD, 2006.

Lechner, Norbert. "A Disenchantment Called Postmodernism." *boundary 2. The Postmodernism Debate in Latin America* 20.3 (1993): 122–139.

Lolo, Eduardo. "José Martí y los niños de todas las edades." *Caribe: Revista de Cultura y Literatura* 4.1 (2001): 24–39.

———. *Mar de Espuma: Martí y la literatura infantil*. Miami: Ediciones Universal, 1995.

López Astudillo, Sandra Elisabeth. "Gioconda Belli: con palabra de mujer." *Encuentro* 35.65 (2003):102–129.

López Terrero, Liana. "Notas sobre el estilo martiano en *La edad de oro*." *La Universidad de La Habana* 235 (1989): 131–142.

Lucas, Ann Lawson, ed. *The Presence of the Past in Children's Literature*. Westport, Connecticut: Praeger, 2003.

Lurie, Alison. *Don't Tell the Grown-ups: Subversive Children's Literature*. Boston: Little, Brown and Company, 1990.

Lyra, Carmen (María Isabel Carvajal). *Cuentos de mi tía Panchita*. San José, Costa Rica: Legado, 2005.

Machado, Ana María, and Graciela Montes. *Literatura infantil: Creación, censura y resistencia*. Buenos Aires: Sudamericana, 2003.

Madrigal Abarca, Marta. "El folclor y la tradición oral en *Los cuentos de mi tía Panchita* de Carmen Lyra." MA thesis. University of Costa Rica, 1996.

Maldonado Denis, Manuel. "Martí y Fanon." *Cuadernos Americanos* 185 (1972): 189–202.

March, Kathleen N. "Gioconda Belli: The Erotic Politics of the Great Mother." *Monographic Review/Revista Monográfica* 6 (1990): 245–257.

Martí, José. *La edad de oro*. San José, Costa Rica: Editorial San Judas Tadeo, 1993.

Martínez, Fabiola. "¿Por qué expulsaron a Cocorí?" *La Nación Suplemento Viva* 24 April 2003: 1.

Martínez, Zulma Nelly. "Entrevista: Manlio Argueta." *Hispamérica: Revista de Literatura* 14.42 (1985): 41–54.

Martínez S., Mauricio. "Costarricense del siglo." *La Nación* 1 December 1999.

Mathews, Daniel. "Martí y los niños." *Espéculo* 9 (1998). 15 March 2007 <http://www.ucm.ed/info/especulo/numero9/marti.html>.

Matute, Rónald. "Racismo en la mente." *La Nación* 28 April 2003: 18A.

Mayorga, Armando. "Matar a un ruiseñor." *La Nación* 23 April 2003: 15.

McDonald, Dlia. "Un pez y un pájaro pueden enamorarse, pero ¿dónde harán su nido?" 1 July 2003 <http://www.clubdelibros.com/archicocoridelia.htm>.

McGillis, Roderick, ed. *Voices of the Other: Children's Literature and the Postcolonial Context*. New York: Garland Publishing, Inc., 1999.

Méndez Garita, María Isabel. "De mariposas amarillas como el sol." Paper presented 25 September 2003. Instituto de México: San José, Costa Rica. 10 May 2007 <http://www.carlosrubioescritor.com/joomla/index.php?option=com_content&task=view&id=33&Itemid=47>.

———. "Ese hilo que se visibiliza y es terso." *La Nación Suplemento Ancora* 6 September 2003. 10 May 2007 <http://www.carlosrubioescritor.com/joomla/index.php?option=com_content&task=view&id=24&Itemid=50>.

———. "Para recrear la auténtica Navidad." *La Nación Suplemento Ancora* 2 December 2001. 10 May 2007 <http://www.carlosrubioescritor.com/joomla/index.php?option=com_content&task=view&id=40&Itemid=56>.

Mickenberg, Julia L. *Learning from the Left: Children's Literature, the Cold War, and Radical Politics in the United States*. New York: Oxford University Press, 2006.

Mignolo, Walter D. *Local Histories/Global Designs: Coloniality, Subaltern Knowledges, and Border Thinking*. Princeton: Princeton University Press, 2000.

———. *The Idea of Latin America*. Malden, MA: Blackwell Publishing, 2005.

Milan Arias, Claudia M. "Rescuing Historical Memory: An Interview with Manlio Argueta." *Ciberletras* 8 (2002): 1–5. 25 July 2008 <http://www.lehman.cuny.edu/ciberletras/v08/arias.html>.

Miller-Lachmann, Lyn, ed. *Once Upon a Cuento*. Willimantic, CT: Curbstone Press, 2003.

Molina Jiménez, Iván. "De cómo Tía Panchita inquietó a un imperio." *Semanario Universidad* 3–9 February 1999: 17.

———. *Costarricense por dicha: Identidad nacional y cambio cultural en Costa Rica durante los siglos XIX y XX*. San José, Costa Rica: Editorial de la Universidad de Costa Rica, 2005.

Mondol, Mijail. "Diálogo y marginalidad en *Cocorí*." *Káñina* 28. Número especial. (2004): 41–47.

Morera Salas, Marta. "Conociendo la literatura infantil en los cuentos de Carlos Rubio." *Temas de Nuestra América* 16 (1991).

Morrison, Ronald D. "Remembering and Recovering *Goblin Market* in Rosario Ferré's 'Pico Rico, Mandorico.'" *Critique* 41.4 (2000): 365–379.

Moyano, Pilar. "Utopía/Distopía: La desmitificación de la revolución sandinista en la narrativa de Gioconda Belli." *Ixquic: Revista Hispánica Internacional de Análisis y Creación* 4 (February 2003): 16–24.

Mullen, Edward. "Interpreting Puerto Rico's Cultural Myths: Rasario Ferré and Manuel Ramos Otero." *The Americas Review* 17.3–4 (1989): 88–97.

Muñoz B., Kattia. "Carlos Rubio, el mago de los cuentos." *Ojo, mirada a la actualidad* 3.49 (22 September–6 October 2003): 18–19. 10 May 2007 <http://www.carlosrubioescritor.com/joomla/index.php?option=com_content&task=view&id=35&Itemid=49>.

Ng, Leibi. "El sueño de Mecho." *Imaginaria* 36 (2000). 2 June 2007 <http://www.imaginaria.com.ar/03/6/ng2_b.htm>.

Nikolajeva, Maria. *From Mythic to Linear: Time in Children's Literature*. Lanham, MD: The Children's Literature Association and the Scarecrow Press, Inc., 2000.

Norton, Donna. *Multicultural Children's Literature: Through the Eyes of Many Children*. Upper Saddle River, New Jersey: Prentice-Hall, Inc., 2001.

Ordóñez, Jaime. "Primero fue Marcos: La falacia de la literatura pura." *La Nación* 24 May 2003: 19A.

Osa, Osayimwense. *African Children's and Youth Literature*. New York: Twayne, 1995.

Ovares, Flora, et al. *La casa paterna: Escritura y nación en Costa Rica*. San José, Costa Rica: Editorial de la Universidad de Costa Rica, 1993.

Oviedo, Lucrecia. *Joaquín Gutiérrez: Novelista*. San José, Costa Rica: Editorial Costa Rica, 1993.

Pacheco, Abel. "Por qué no Cocorí." *La Nación* 26 April 2003.

Palmer-López, Sandra M. "Los 'Cuentos Maravillosos' de *Sonatinas* de Rosario Ferré: Re-escritura femenina, feminista del cuento de hadas." *Revista de Estudios Hispánicos* 26.1 (1999): 31–46.

Paz, Octavio. *El Laberinto de la soledad*. Mexico: Cuadernos Americanos, 1950.

Pérez, Hebert. "Martí, Race, and Cuban Identity." *Monthly Review: An Independent Socialist Magazine* 55.6 (2003): 19–32.

Pérez-Yglesias, María. "Cocorí es mi hijo menor . . . : La expresividad del narrador en la novela infantil de Joaquín Gutiérrez Mangel." *Káñina* 7.2 (1983): 9–19.

———. "Entre la polémica y el espectáculo: Cocorí mi negro lindo." *Káñina* 28. Número especial (2004): 47–54.

Peris Peris, Cecilia. "Rosario Ferré: La redefinición de la literatura infantil a través de 'Amalia,' 'El regalo' y 'La muñeca menor.'" Proyecto Ensayo Hispánico, 2006. 21 March 2007 <http://www.ensayistas.org/folosofos/puertorico/ferre/peris/introd.htm>.

Pineda Lima, Sonia. "Bibliografía sobre Joaquín Gutiérrez Mangel 1918–2000." *Káñina* 28. Número especial (2004): 91–116.

Powell, Lorein. "Lectura (en crísis) de tres obras racistas" Licenciatura Thesis. Universidad Nacional, 1985.

Pozo Campos, Esther. "La composición en tres cuentos de *La edad de oro.*" *La Universidad de La Habana* 235 (1989): 119–130.

Prasad, Anshuman, ed. *Postcolonial Theory and Organizational Analysis: A Critical Engagement.* New York: Palgrave Macmillan, 2003.

Pratt, Linda, and Janice J. Beaty. *Transcultural Children's Literature.* Upper Saddle River, NJ: Merrill, 1999.

Preble-Niemi, Oralia. "Gioconda Belli" in *Modern Spanish American Poets: Second Series.* Ed. María A. Salgado. Detroit, MI: Gale, 2004: 26–33.

Puleo, Augustus. "The Intersection of Race, Sex, Gender and Class in a Short Story of Rosario Ferré." *Studies in Short Fiction* 32 (1995): 227–236.

Quesada Pacheco, Miguel A. *Nuevo Diccionario de Costarriqueñismos.* 3rd ed. Cartago, Costa Rica: Editorial Tecnológica de Costa Rica, 2001.

Quesada Soto, Alvaro. "Nación y enajenación: Modelos de identidad en la literatura costarricense," *Filología y Lingüística* 21.2 (1995): 41–57.

———. *Uno y los otros.* San José, Costa Rica: Editorial de la Universidad de Costa Rica, 2002.

Rabbit Play Trik Pahn Hanaasi. Belize City, Belize: Di Bileez Kriol Projek, 1997.

Ramírez, Paola. "Negrito maromero y aventurero." *La República* 3 July 1999: 5B.

Ramos, Lilia. "El Encantador 'Cocorí' de Gutiérrez." *Excelsior* 1 February 1978: 2.

Retana, Marco. "Los cuentos de me tía Panchita." *La República* 15 July 1980: 9.

Rhoden, Laura Barbas. "The Quest for the Mother in the Novels of Gioconda Belli." *Letras Femeninas* 27 (2000): 81–97.

Richards, Jeffrey, ed. *Imperialism and Juvenile Literature.* Manchester: Manchester University Press, 1989.

Ríos, Lara. *Algodón de azúcar.* San José, Costa Rica: Farben Grupo Editorial Norma, 1994.

———. *Aventuras de Dora la lora y Chico Perico.* San José, Costa Rica: Farben Grupo Editorial Norma, 2004.

———. *El círculo de fuego blanco.* San José, Costa Rica: Farben Grupo Editorial Norma, 2000.

———. *Mo.* San José, Costa Rica: Farben Grupo Editorial Norma, 2005.

———. *La música de Paul.* San José, Costa Rica: Farben Grupo Editorial Norma, 2001.

———. *Nuevas aventuras de Dora la lora y Chico Perico*. San José, Costa Rica: Farben Grupo Editorial Norma, 2005.

———. *Pantalones cortos*. San José, Costa Rica: Farben Grupo Editorial Norma, 1996.

———. *Pantalones largos*. San José, Costa Rica: Farben Grupo Editorial Norma, 1995.

———. *Verano de colores*. San José, Costa Rica: Farben Grupo Editorial Norma, 1994.

Robles Mohs, Ivonne. "*Cocorí*: una polifonía textual." *Káñina* 28. Número especial (2004): 61–66.

Rodríguez, Antonio Orlando. *Panorama histórico de la literatura infantil en América Latina y el Caribe*. CERLALC, 1992.

Rodríguez, Ileana, ed. *The Latin American Subaltern Studies Reader*. Durham: Duke University Press, 2001.

Rodríguez, Luis Ricardo. "Review of *Escuela de hechicería*." *La Nación* 6 November 1996. 10 May 2007 <http://www.carlosrubioescritor.com/joomla/index.php?option=com_content&task=view&id=39&Itemid=55>.

Rodríguez Jiménez, Olga M. "¿Hay elementos racistas en *Cocorí*?" *Káñina* 28. Número especial (2004): 55–61.

Rodríguez Valle, Nieves. "El coyote en la literatura de tradición oral." 1 June 2007   <http://www.rlp.culturaspopulares.org/textos%20V-1/07-Rodriguez.pdf>.

Rojas, Margarita, and Flora Ovares. *100 años de literatura costarricense*. San José, Costa Rica: Farben Grupo Editorial Norma, 1995.

Rubio, Carlos. "Cocorí y la lectura obligatoria." *Káñina* 28. Número especial (2004): 67–72.

———. *Escuela de hechicería: Matrícula abierta*. San José, Costa Rica: Farben Grupo Editorial Norma, 1996.

———. *El libro de la Navidad*. Heredia, Costa Rica: Editorial Universidad Nacional, 2001.

———. *La mujer que se sabía todos los cuentos*. Grupo Editorial Norma, 2003.

———. *Papá es un campeón*. San José, Costa Rica: Grupo Editorial Norma, 2006.

———. *Pedro y su teatrino maravilloso*. San José, Costa Rica: Editorial Costa Rica, 1992.

———. Web page. 10 May 2007 <http://www.carlosrubioescritor.com>.

———. *Queremos jugar*. 2nd ed. San José, Costa Rica: Farben Grupo Editorial Norma, 2006.

———. *La vida entre los labios*. San José, Costa Rica: Editorial Costa Rica, 1985.

Sánchez, Constantino. "Review of *Escuela de hechicería, matrícula abierta*." *Revista Abracadabra* 3. 10 May 2007 <http://www.carlosrubioescritor.com/joomla/index.php?option=com_content&task=view&id=38&Itemid=54>.

Sánchez M., Álvaro. "El negro en la literatura costarricense." *El negro en Costa Rica*. Eds. Quince Duncan and Carlos Meléndez. 11th ed. San José, Costa Rica: Editorial Costa Rica, 2005.

Santos Pasamontes, Ignacio. "Un viejo tigre nigromante es el 'papá' del negrito Cocorí." *La Nación* (14 October 1984): 6C.

Schade, George. "La novelística de Joaquín Gutiérrez." *Brecha* 2.7 (September/August 1957): 11.

Schon, Isabel, and Sarah Corona Berkin. *Introducción a la literatura infantil y juvenil*. Newark: International Reading Association, 1996.

Schultz de Mantovani, Fryda. "Prólogo." *La edad de oro*. By José Martí. San Salvador: Departamento Editorial Ministerio de Cultura, 1955.

Serna Arnaiz, Mercedes. "Estética e ideología en *La edad de oro* de José Martí: 'La muñeca negra.'" *Notas y Estudios Filológicos* 9 (1994): 193–213.

Sloan, Cynthia A. "Caricature, Parody, and Dolls: How to Play at Deconstructing and (Re-)Constructing Female Identity in Rosario Ferré's *Papeles de Pandora*." *Pacific Coast Philology* 35.1 (2000): 35–48.

Sommer, Doris. *Foundational Fictions: The National Romances of Latin America*. Berkeley: University of California Press, 1991.

Sparisci Lovicelli, Luciana. "Lectura Retórica de *Cocorí*." *Káñina* 26.1 (2002):15–21.

———. "¿Te . . . acuerdas . . . de mi flor? Lo retórico-sentencioso en el diálogo con el negro cantor." *Káñina* 28. Número especial (2004): 73–79.

Spivak, Gayatri Chakravorty. "Can the Subaltern Speak?" *The Post-Colonial Studies Reader*. Eds. B. Ashcroft, G. Griffiths, and H. Tiffin. London and New York: Routledge, 1995.

Stephens, John. *Language and Ideology in Children's Fiction*. London: Longman, 1992.

Swain, J. O. "Some Costa Rican Writers as Topics for Research." *Hispania* 22.2 (1939): 183–188.

Toral Alemañ, Begoña. "Entre Puerto Rico y Estados Unidos: Entrevista a Rosario Ferré." *Caribe* 3.2 (2000): 51–62.

Torres Rioseco, Arturo. "Estudios Literarios: José Martí: El hombre." *Hispania* 5.5 (November 1922): 282–285.

Ubiñas Renville, Juan Guaroa. *La ciguapa dominicana*. Santo Domingo: Editorial Letra Gráfica, 2001.

Ugalde, Evelyn. "Homenaje a Lara Ríos." 10 May 2007 <http://www.clubdelibros.com/archilararios.htm>.

Ugalde, Sharon Keefe. "Review: Process, Identity, and Learning to Read: Female Writing and Feminist Criticism in Latin America Today." *Latin American Research Review* 24.1 (1989): 222–232.

Valembois, Victor. "Cocorí, de discriminante a discriminado." *Revista Comunicación ITCR* 12.1&2 (2003). 25 July 2008 <http://www.itcr.ac.cr/revistacomunicacion/Vol_13_N1y2/cocori.htm>.

Vargas, Aura Rosa. "Los estilos de reproducción de *Cocorí*." *Revista de la Universidad de Costa Rica* 26 (1969): 107–114.

Vargas Llosa, Mario. *Conversación en la catedral*. Spain: Seix Barral, 1969.

Vásquez Vargas, Magdalena. "Te conozco, Cocorí: Un aporte a la caracterización del niño como protagonista." *Káñina* 28. Número especial (2004): 79–84.

Vazquez, Doris M. "Rosario Ferré: Una cuentista puertorriquéna (sic) contemporánea" (*A Contemporary Puerto Rican Storyteller*). Yale–New Haven Teachers Institute. March 18, 2007 <http://www.yale.edu/ynhti/curriculum/units/1987/1/87.01.09.x.htm>.

Víquez Guzmán, Benedicto. *Los cuentos de mi tía Panchita (Modelo, género e interpretación)*. Thesis. University of Costa Rica, 1976. San José: University of Costa Rica, 1986.

Webster, Joan Parker. *Teaching Through Culture: Strategies for Reading and Responding to Young Adult Literature*. Houston: Arte Público Press, 2002.

Wilkins, Lawrence. *Primeros [segundos] pasos en español*. New York: Henry Holt and Company, 1932–1933.

Zornado, Joseph L. *Inventing the Child: Culture, Ideology, and the Story of Childhood*. New York: Garland Publishing, 2001.

Index

About the Author

Ann B. González is originally from North Carolina. She has a B.A. in English from the University of North Carolina Chapel Hill, and an M.A. and Ph.D. in Comparative Literature from the University of South Carolina. She spent eight years teaching English and American literature at the University of Costa Rica (1980–1988). Currently, she is Associate Chair of the Department of Languages and Culture Studies and Professor of Spanish and Latin American Studies at the University of North Carolina Charlotte. Her special field of interest is Spanish American literature, particularly Central American fiction. Her first book published by Fairleigh Dickinson University Press, *Sí pero no*, was a postcolonial analysis of the work of Costa Rican novelist Fabián Dobles. Her research on Central American children's literature grew out of a course on Hispanic children's literature that she developed and now regularly offers at both the undergraduate and graduate levels at UNC Charlotte, as well as from her experiences reading stories in both English and Spanish to her own children.